D0841633

FRIENDSHIP

The Rowman & Littlefield Empowering You series is aimed to help you, as a young adult, deal with important topics that you, your friends, or family might be facing. Whether you are looking for answers about certain illnesses, social issues, or personal problems, the books in this series provide you with the most up-to-date information. Throughout each book you will also find stories from other teenagers to provide personal perspectives on the subject.

FRIENDSHIP

Insights and Tips for Teenagers

Jean Rawitt

ROWMAN & LITTLEFIELD
Lanham • Boulder • New York • London

Published by Rowman & Littlefield
An imprint of The Rowman & Littlefield Publishing Group, Inc.
4501 Forbes Boulevard, Suite 200, Lanham, Maryland 20706
www.rowman.com

86-90 Paul Street, London EC2A 4NE, United Kingdom

British Library Cataloguing in Publication Information Available

Library of Congress Cataloging-in-Publication Data

Name: Rawitt, Jean, 1952–, author.
Title: Friendship : insights and tips for teenagers / Jean Rawitt.
Description: Lanham : Rowman & Littlefield, [2022] | Series: Empowering you | Includes bibliographical references and index. | Audience: Ages 13–17 | Audience: Grades 10–12 | Summary: "In this age of social media, where so many friendships exist almost solely online, this book explores the greater meaning of friendship as an enduring and emotionally important area of life. It is a valuable resource for teenagers who are struggling to make friends, are in a toxic friendship, or just want to build more meaningful relationships"—Provided by publisher.
Identifiers: LCCN 2021036221 (print) | LCCN 2021036222 (ebook) | ISBN 9781538152874 (paperback) | ISBN 9781538152881 (epub)
Subjects: LCSH: Friendship—Juvenile literature.
Classification: LCC HM1161 .R39 2022 (print) | LCC HM1161 (ebook) | DDC 177/.62—dc23
LC record available at https://lccn.loc.gov/2021036221
LC ebook record available at https://lccn.loc.gov/2021036222

CONTENTS

INTRODUCTION

You Are Not Alone

It seems so easy—friends are friends, aren't they? Everyone has friends, don't they? So why a book on friendship?

Friendship can be simple, and friendship can be complicated. Some people find making friends effortless; they don't know how they do it, but they seem to make friends without even trying. For others, making friends seems difficult, intimidating, or even impossible. They may find themselves tongue-tied when talking with strangers, or reluctant to approach someone they don't know at a party. They may be too shy to say hi to an unfamiliar person, or afraid they might look silly or overeager. They may have been hurt by someone they thought was a friend, and are wary of it happening again. But most people want to have friends, and those barriers to friendship can be overcome. As we explore further in this book, we will find that there are ways to think about friendship—even some tools—which can help anyone become more comfortable making friends, keeping friends, and valuing what friendship can bring to our lives.

Friendships have provided some of the richest relationships of my life, and they continue to do so, as I hope they will for as long as I live. Perhaps because they mean so much to me, I've thought a lot about the various friendships I've had throughout my life, what they meant at different times, what they offered me, and—hopefully—what those relationships meant to the friends with whom I shared them. As I started to think more about it, and began talking with others about what friendship means to them, I found that many of the discussions led back to what friendship meant to people when they were young, and how their friendships developed and deepened—and, sometimes, ended. I knew I wanted to explore that further, and find out from young people themselves what *they* thought about friendship, and what they could tell me about what friendship meant to them, how their friendships developed, and what joys—and difficulties—they found in friendship.

While for many young people friendships seem to happen naturally, for others making friends is hard—and a cause for anxiety and stress. As Ben, one young man I spoke with, put it, "There are tons of kids who don't have friends, and want to make friends, but don't know how to do it, or are afraid of trying to do it." But, he continued, "Everyone is capable of making friends. Some kids just don't have the confidence to go out and make friends." And it is my hope that some of the insights and tips included in this book will make it easier for those kids to find that making friends is not only possible for them, but a chance for them to find more enjoyment and comfort than they expected.

In writing this book, I asked young people from around the country what friendship meant to them, and I noticed that their answers mirrored remarkably straightforward, and similar, feelings. Henry, a young man in Washington, DC, told me, "A friend is someone that you like, someone that you get along with, someone who has interests you share." Jordana, in New York, said that, to her, "friendship means a group who have a bond together, who can trust each other, who can rely on each other for different things." From Judith, I heard that friendship meant "Relationships with people that I'm close with, people I can trust." And Tali told me, "A friend is someone who you can always lean on, no matter what, and they're always there for you when you need them the most." It was clear that, to these young people, there were qualities they hoped for and expected from friendship, and these were qualities I wanted to delve into further.

With the help of the many young people I had the pleasure of interviewing for this book, I have been able to explore how friendships are made, the benefits of friendships, different types of friendships, how one can recognize a true friend, how to recognize and deal with a failed or toxic friendship, and what we learn from friendship. These young people spoke openly about their thoughts and feelings about friendships, their difficulties and their joys, and it is their voices I hope will resonate with you, the reader. Thanks to the young people who shared their insights and stories with me, I have been able to include ideas and suggestions I hope many young people will find useful throughout their lives as they make, and keep, good friends.

Part One

What Is Friendship?

I

WHAT IS FRIENDSHIP, AND WHY IS IT IMPORTANT?

"Friends are the keystone to my happiness."—Ben, age eighteen

The *Merriam-Webster Dictionary* defines a friend as "one attached to another by affection or esteem" or "a favored companion." It describes friendship as "the state of being a friend" and "a friendly feeling or disposition."[1] These seem to be simple definitions, but let's look deeper and think about what friendship really is, and why it is so important in our lives.

The history of friendship has been documented over many thousands of years. One of the very earliest historical documentations of friendship can be found in the ancient *Epic of Gilgamesh*, originally written on clay tablets sometime between 2750 and 2500 BCE. Thought by some to be the oldest written story, the epic tells of Gilgamesh, a king of Sumeria, who prayed to a goddess to create someone to be his equal, "as like him as his own reflection, his second self." The goddess then created a comrade for him out of clay and brought him to life. Enkidu, her creation, then became Gilgamesh's closest companion, following him and sharing adventures and hardship, and sealing their friendship for life.[2]

The Old Testament documents numerous friendships of enduring poignancy. In the Book of Samuel, the example of the loving friendship between David and Jonathan tells of how Jonathan, son of King Saul, saved David from being killed by the king, even though David stood to inherit all that was Jonathan's legacy.[3] In the Book of Ruth, another book of the Old Testament, the words of Ruth, speaking to her mother-in-law, Naomi, tell of a heartfelt and cross-generational friendship: "Entreat me not to leave, or to return from following after thee: for whither thou goest, I will go; and where you lodgest, I will lodge; thy people will be my people, and thy God my God."[4] Another example can be found in the Book of Job, where there is this wonderful description of friendship: "When Job's three friends, Eliphaz the Temanite, Bildad the Shuhite and Zophar the Naamathite, heard about all the troubles that had come upon him, they set out from their homes and met together by agreement to go and sympathize with him and comfort him."[5]

There are many other ancient literary depictions and explications of friendships. The Greek epic *The Aeneid* by Virgil, written between 29 and 19 BCE, includes the legendary friendship between Aeneas, the hero of the epic, and his faithful companion Achates, who remains with him throughout his years of travel. The Roman statesman and scholar Marcus Tullius Cicero wrote an entire essay in 44 BCE called "How to Be a Friend," in which he wrote, "What could be sweeter than to have someone you can dare to talk to about everything as if you were speaking to yourself? How could you enjoy the good times of life if you didn't have someone who was as happy about your good fortune as you are?"[6] And even Egyptian hieroglyphs, the pictorial illustrations found in tombs, depict what are believed to be important friendships. When translating ancient letters found in excavations in Deir El-Medina, the Valley of Artisans in Egypt, scholar Deborah Sweeney found writings thousands of years old stressing the importance of friendship, in which the writer tells how friends should care for one another, help one another, and comply with one another's requests.[7] Native American, African, Asian, and East Asian traditional tales all include significant depictions of friendship. Almost certainly, friendship has been important—even necessary—throughout human history.

Closer to our own times, literary friendships have entertained people for hundreds of years. William Shakespeare created brilliantly complex pairs of friends, such as Horatio and Hamlet in *Hamlet*, Hermia and Helena in *A Midsummer Night's Dream*, and Rosalind and Celia in *As You Like It*.[8] Mark Twain's wonderful depiction of the friendship between Tom Sawyer and Huckleberry Finn in *The Adventures of Tom Sawyer*, Jane Austen's warm and delightful friendship between Elizabeth Bennett and Charlotte Lucas in *Pride and Prejudice*, Sancho Panza and Don Quixote in Cervantes's classic *Don Quixote*, and the March sisters in Louisa May Alcott's *Little Women* are enduring and much loved examples of very different friendships during very different times, but no less fresh and appealing today.

All of these ancient, mythic, and literary examples teach us about how friendship can encompass loyalty, empathy, and deep devotion, but also treachery, misunderstanding, and ruin. These tales, whether told and retold year after year, acted on stage, or read alone or aloud to others, give us a framework in which to understand the meaning and endurance of friendship, as well as a guide to what we may expect, and hope for, in friendship.

But why did this very special human relationship develop? Perhaps friendship evolved out of necessity. The earliest humans must have needed companions to assist them in hunting the great beasts on whom their sustenance depended. One person could not successfully hunt alone; they depended on one or more others to help with the kill, the butchering, the protection from dangers. Women were dependent on other women to help with birth, with child rearing, perhaps with security when the men were away hunting. Humans evolved dependent on others. I like to speculate that humans began to favor certain people over others, to trust certain people over others, and, in fact, to feel emotional closeness to certain people over others. And that is the essence of friendship.

What is it about friendship that most of us enjoy so much? What is it that makes friendship so important? Friends make us feel good. They make us feel good about ourselves, and they make us feel good about things in general. Friends can see the best in us, and

reflect those things back at us when we might not see them ourselves. One wonderful image, attributed to Aristotle, the ancient
Greek philosopher and scientist, is that "a friend is one who holds a
mirror up to us."[9] Friends can encourage us, and friends can inspire
us to reach for things we might not otherwise strive for. And a true
friend will be honest with us, even when we may not want to hear
the truth.

Friendship encompasses other virtues as well. Friends are loyal
to each other, treat each other with affection and generosity; friends
are empathetic to each other's feelings, and friends are forgiving of
each other's flaws and mistakes.

Friends share life with each other; they enhance the fun times
and comfort us when times are hard or sad. They allow us to show
our authentic self to them when we may choose to hide some parts
of ourselves from others. Friendships enrich our lives. They offer us
a space in which we can let down our guard, and feel we can truly
be ourselves; they can offer relief from circumstances and environments that may cause us stress or discomfort. Friendship can give us
the feeling that someone always "has our back," is an ally in our
life, and is someone we can turn to no matter what.

Those needs, those feelings, encapsulate what friendship is.
While it may be true that some rare individuals can live, perhaps
even successfully, without friendships, most people have friends.
Some people may have more friends than others; that can depend on
their personalities, their environment, and their exposure to the
world outside their home. But generally, people form friendships
with those with whom they share common interests and feel a personal, often emotional, connection; they know they can trust them
with their innermost feelings, and they can share experiences. It is
that connection, that inclination to share—whether experiences or
thoughts or feelings, or all of those things—that sums up what
friendship is.

While some friendships seem effortless, or seem to happen instantly, other friendships take time to develop. Some friendships do
not start out as friendships but rather as acquaintanceships, or a sort
of casual companionship, and develop into something deeper and

more significant over time. Developing a friendship can take work, and maintaining a friendship can take intention and effort. You may have to go out of your way to ensure that you have opportunities to develop a closer bond with someone, whether by arranging to meet, or call, or find other ways to get to know each other better. You may even have to ignore a perceived slight. It can take work over a considerable amount of time to maintain and deepen such a connection.

Friendships can also change over time. They can become stronger, or weaker. They can end entirely—whether by intention or by circumstance. Such an ending can be sad, or it can be thorny, or even hurtful. Friendships have different meanings, and take on different forms, according to different stages of life. A six-year-old's friendships are very different from those of a twelve-year-old, which may be very different from those of a young adult. But all of those friendships can be authentic, meaningful, and beneficial—and even a six-year-old's friendship can turn into a lifetime relationship.

The benefits of friendship have lasting social, emotional, and psychological impact. Friends can have a positive effect on a teenager's self-esteem by providing companionship and support, especially when teens are beginning to widen their social network and activities beyond their childhood circle and their own family. Friendship can help young people develop lifelong skills necessary for interaction in the adult world. In an article in the *New York Times*, author Lydia Denworth writes, "Friendship is where kids build social skills—companionship, trust, loyalty, reciprocity and reconciliation—that they can only learn from peer relationships. These are muscles they need to strengthen for adulthood."[10] And a study carried out by researchers at the University of Virginia in Charlottesville reported that teenagers with close friendships tended to be more able to adapt to stress, were happier, and were likely to do better academically, as well as having higher self-esteem and being more assertive.[11]

And, it turns out, friendship can have physical benefits as well. For example, a study highlighted in *Psychological Science* shows that boys who spend more time with friends as children tend to have lower blood pressure and have a healthier body mass index (BMI) as adults.[12] And the results of a 2016 study suggested that having social networks and social integration during adolescence had a positive effect on healthy metabolic and cardiovascular functioning into adulthood.[13]

Young people themselves seem to know this intuitively. As Judith, a young woman I interviewed, says, "Friends are such a big part of my life that it's very important to me." To Sylvia, "Friendship means having someone there for you, someone you can talk to, hang out with. And that's incredibly important to me." And as Grace articulated eloquently, "Friendship is building bonds with people, and knowing that you'll stay connected to them, and that they'll be there for you and that you can be there for them. It's just a deeper human connection, I think, that everyone needs. And I think that it's a really important part of life for every kid, because, obviously, even if your family is great, you have to get out there to meet new people, and to see different perspectives."

Hattie, a young New Yorker, told me that to her friendship meant "feeling comfortable with that person; not always having to say the most politically correct things. Friends don't have to wear their public persona with each other. You have confidence in your friends, and they give you a sense of security. Even if you fight, you know you can make up after that. Friendship means being honest with each other—you can say to a friend, 'That's a ridiculous idea.' And if you can't, then your relationship is just superficial. With a friend, you can feel comfortable saying something they might not like. And, it may sound sappy, but if your friend gets hurt, you feel it."

And Ben, a young man who has had the unusual experience of living both in New York and in England, where he goes to school, found that friendship was deeply important to him, primarily because his life is spent in two countries so far apart. When we spoke, he had some very eloquent and heartfelt things to say about what friendship means to him.

BEN'S STORY

When I was eight, I started boarding school in England. My parents were in the United States, and so my friends became the ones who were really important to me, maybe more important for me than they were for some of the other guys, especially since my parents were in a different country. In a way, they became my family. I think I struggled a lot more than some of my mates who had parents close by.

I had relationships in school that were quite close; they were really good friends. I'm still best friends with some of them, and have been since the time we were eight, when we first met at school. I think making friends depends on the situations you're in; the friends I made through school are mostly guys in my dorm, or some good mates I made through mutual friends. And although most of my close friends share my interests, I do have some friends, not as close as my best friends, but there are other guys who are really nice, really genuine, but not really that similar to me—and I can always have good, interesting conversations with them.

For me, friends are the keystone to my happiness. They take your mind off things that are troubling you, things that are causing you stress. I always feel that my friends will be there for me, help me when I need help, whether it's with schoolwork, sports, or anything else. We always find ways to cooperate. Some of them have a similar personality to me, but some have very different personalities, and that lets me enjoy new things that I wouldn't otherwise enjoy in life. They introduce me to new things—my friends have introduced me to great new food places, they've introduced me to burgers, lobster, other things I might not have known about.

What's important to me is the time spent with them, the way we get along. We crack each other up. What's important is that friends give each other support; they want you to do well, to succeed; they help you reach your goals, they offer you love and support. Someone who doesn't, isn't a friend. I think the proof of friendship is that friends make you feel happy; you always miss them tons when you're away from them; with them, you enjoy everything even more.

My friends are my backbone; they keep me up.

2

THE DIFFERENCE BETWEEN FRIENDSHIP AND OTHER RELATIONSHIPS

There are countless variations on relationships among humans. Think of the many kinds of human connections that exist. There are family relations. Neighbors. School acquaintances. Business colleagues. Bunk mates or dorm mates. Mentors and mentees. Counselors and campers. Romantic partners. Teachers and students. Coaches and players. Teammates. Musical partners. And then there are friends. What is it about friendship that differs from other interpersonal relationships?

One way friendship differs from other relationships is that we generally choose our friends; although friendship can start from a chance encounter, it develops because we *want* it to—we choose to continue the relationship, and we usually do that because we enjoy it. Whether it is young kids deciding to play together (when they are old enough to decide for themselves) or older kids choosing to meet after school or sit together at lunch, friendships develop because we make a decision to proceed. We cannot choose our families; we rarely have a choice in teachers, or counselors, or team members. We can sometimes choose musical partners, mentors or advisors, or business colleagues, and we usually choose romantic partners, although historically—and still in some cultures—the choice of romantic partner is made by parents, family, or trusted matchmakers. But, almost universally, friendship is a personal choice. Although a friendship may develop between very young kids when their mothers decide to pair them on a playdate, it is generally up to the kids themselves to create or continue that friendship—or not.

Friendships differ from family relationships because while we choose our friends, we do not choose our family, our kin. Our relatives—whether related by blood or marriage—constitute our family, whether we like them or not. While we might not often get to see, or even know, members of our family, they are, and will remain, part of who we are for the whole of our lives. While we might be closer or more distant with them at different times, the basic relationship remains the same. And although some people have close friendships with kinfolk, we cannot make kin of our friends, other than through marriage or adoption.

Then there are casual acquaintances. In a recent article in the *New York Times*, Alex Williams explains, "Friends generally fall into tiers, like those old food-pyramid posters in the school cafeteria, except in this case, the tiny triangle at the pinnacle is where all the good stuff is, your best friends who provide the most nourishment. The broad base of the pyramid represents the acquaintances, the kinda-friends, the friends of friends and amiable whoevers."[1] Casual acquaintances fill our lives, and they matter, but not in the same way that friends do.

Casual acquaintances are generally people with whom we interact sporadically, whether in school, in the community, or in other activities. You may have a casual acquaintanceship with someone who plays in the same school orchestra and with whom you chat before class. Or you may ride the bus with someone every day and say hi, but you don't visit each other's homes. We can have many casual acquaintances in our lives, but we feel differently about them than we do our friends. We usually don't confide in them as we do with our friends, or spend as much time with them, or expect that they will be a significant part of our life for a long time to come. However, casual acquaintances can become friends, and—though perhaps more rarely—even good friendships can fade until two former friends are really only acquaintances.

Somewhere between casual acquaintances and real friends may lie some relationships like teammates, bunk mates, lab or study partners, or fellow club members. You may be closer to them than you are with casual acquaintances, usually because you have more in common and more to talk about than you do with casual acquaintances, yet you may not feel that special closeness that you do with a real friend. But that kind of relationship can certainly flourish over time and deepen into a true friendship.

Another interpersonal relationship that can be very important is that between a mentor and the person to whom they give mentorship, known as a mentee. A mentor, as defined by the *Funk & Wagnalls Dictionary*, is "a wise and trusted teacher or guide."[2] For some young people developing an interest in a particular subject or art form, a teacher or an advisor becomes a mentor, providing them with guidance and support as they develop their interest or skills further. A camp counselor, a religious leader, a coach, or anyone else, though usually someone older and with considerable experience and expertise, can become a mentor who helps you focus and enhance your interest or skills. Sometimes a mentor-mentee relationship can last for years and become extremely close, but because there is usually a considerable difference in age and experience, that relationship is most often considered something more formal than a friendship.

How are romantic partners different from friends? While one can say that we choose our friends, some people feel that a romantic partner is less a choice than a given—that the attraction we feel for a romantic partner is not something we control. Many of the same qualities must be present for both types of relationship to be successful: trust, reciprocity, and respect, for example. But while a close friendship can be lifelong and intense, the deep attachment and special bond of a romantic relationship usually entail added elements of physical attraction and mutual decision making that transcend those of friendship. A friend can become a romantic partner—sometimes after a period where the friendship deepens until a spark of physical attraction seems to take over and change the relationship. And sometimes a romantic relationship loses that spark but still retains the deep affection, and the romantic partner remains as a friend.

All these social relationships, and the many others that exist, are an integral part of our enjoyment and engagement in life. They each have different, if unspoken, rules of behavior—for instance, while you may run up and hug a friend, you are less likely to do that with a casual acquaintance. These social relationships may have a certain fluidity, where they appear and disappear, or they may change over time. Each has its own values and pleasures, and its own place in our lives. But true friendship may in some ways be the most constant, the least complicated, and the most rewarding social relationship that we have. Most of us genuinely crave warm friendship and thrive within it. Let's explore it further, and try to understand what we can do to make it happen, and make it happen well.

3

TYPES OF FRIENDSHIPS

Friends, casual friends, good friends, best friends. Just as friends don't come in one size, color, or type, friendships are not all the same. When you think of what a friend is, you might think first of someone your own age, your own gender, with similar experiences to yours—in other words, a mirror of yourself. However, there are many different types of friendships, and they function in different ways and serve different roles. Hopefully, you will find yourself with many different kinds of friendships during your life and enjoy the benefits these different relationships bring.

Deep and meaningful friendships can develop between people of different ages. People of different genders can have rewarding friendships that are not necessarily romantic. People can have friends who make an appearance in their lives for only a brief time, and friends can disappear and reappear much later, renewing bonds of long ago. Friends can be related by blood, and valuable friendships can develop with people one has never met face to face. There are even friendships that don't appear in real life but can nevertheless be valuable. What these and other types of friendships share is that for whatever length of time they exist, they are important and meaningful, often deeply rewarding and enjoyable, and engage heartfelt feelings within us that are often kept for a lifetime. Let's take a look at some different types of friendships and explore their meaning and dynamics.

RELATIVES WHO ARE ALSO FRIENDS

We generally think of friends as people outside our family, and indeed that is usually the case. However, for some people, someone who is related to them by blood or marriage (sometimes called kinsmen or kin), especially if it is someone close to them in age, is also a close personal friend. Sometimes these relationships—between siblings, cousins, stepsiblings, or with aunts and uncles—carry, in some ways, an even closer bond than close friendships.

Tali has a cousin with whom she feels friendship as much as kinship. "My cousin Ari, whenever we're together, we hang out—not like cousins, more like friends. We live in different states, so we don't actually get together that often, and we don't have friends in common. But we're both really passionate about theater, so we talk about drama and stuff like that, what's going on in our schools, our drama clubs. And even though we don't know the people the other one is talking about, we kind of feel we know them, because we've heard so much about them. When we're not together we don't really text that much, but we do sometimes FaceTime to catch up. Ari's a year younger than me, but I don't feel the age difference, and it's not uncomfortable that he's a boy—maybe because he's also my cousin. We just feel really connected."

Judith related, "My cousin is also my really close friend. She is younger than me, but we get along really, really well. And I kind of wish she was my sister. The last time I saw her was this summer, in my backyard. We kept socially distanced, but it was so great to see her and spend time with her. I've known her since I was two, when she was a little younger. We would get together a lot, and it's like we were always friends, aside from being cousins. We FaceTime a lot, and sometimes I help her with her homework, or a science experiment. It's great to FaceTime with her while I'm also doing something else, like I can prop the phone up while I'm baking cookies or something, and we just talk and talk. So we FaceTime a lot—I bake a lot."

Grace explained, "My cousins are all a lot older than me; the youngest one, closest to me, is twenty-one. I really love talking to them, we get along great, but I don't think we keep in touch as friends outside of family stuff. We call on birthdays, and see each other when the whole family gets together, but not really outside of that. But I do know kids who are really close friends with their cousins, and actually, I'm a little jealous of them. One of my friends from school spent the whole summer with her cousins, and they're great friends; it always sounded great to me to have someone like that—someone who's family, but even more, your close friend."

Sylvia is another one of those kids who treasures her cousin as a friend, especially because of the unusual circumstance of their first meeting. "I only have two cousins who are at all close to my age," she told me. "And one of them is also really a close friend. She was actually born on the same day as me, in the same year, although she's eight hours older than me. I feel very close to her, like she's a best friend, not just a relation. And it's weird, because I only met her for the first time in February of last year. I'd never seen her in my entire life, and I actually first met her on an airplane. It turned out that we were both going to my great-grandmother's one hundredth birthday party, in Arizona. I had known that I had a cousin who was born on the same day as me, but I'd never met her, and I didn't know that she was going to there. And then, when I was on the airplane going to Phoenix, I saw a girl who walked by with two other kids and her mom, and she looked about my age, and I noticed that she had really cool hair. Then the next day, I went to my great-grandmother's birthday party, and there she was! And then my mom's pulling me over to her, saying, 'This is your cousin Naomi,' and I'm like, *Cool!*, and I blurted out, 'Hey, I saw you on the airplane!' While we were in Phoenix for that week, we spent a huge amount of time together, and just bonded over everything. I couldn't believe that I'd found this new friend, and she turned out to be not only my first cousin whom I'd never met, but almost my twin! We live about four hours away from each other; she lives closer to my grandmother's house, but when we're driving to see my grandmother in Arizona, I can see her house from the freeway. Unfortunately, right after we spent that great week together, the pandemic hit, so I haven't been able to see her any other time in person since then. But we text and FaceTime all the time, and I think I feel closer to her than to anyone."

IMAGINARY FRIENDS

While many small children create an invisible friend,[1] preadolescents and adolescents are less likely to discuss or reveal the presence in their lives of imaginary companions. While children may talk about playing with their invisible friend, or inform their parents of details about them, adolescents may be more likely to create imaginary friends in the confines of their diary or other writings. Social scientists have explored the functions of such invisible companions, looking, for example, at whether such companionship may reflect a greater amount of creativity, and have found that very often the imagined companion was similar to the writer in many aspects and supported the adolescent during the process of developing his or her identity.[2]

I remember my own early experience with—if not an imaginary friend—an unknown friend, a girl I never knew. I'd gone for a picnic with my family, and, wandering away a bit, I found, nestled in a hole in a tree, a handmade doll figure cleverly crafted out of small branches, a bit of cloth, and who knows what else. It charmed me, and I just knew it had been made by another girl and left there for me to find and enjoy. When we packed up to leave, I carefully placed it back in its arboreal hideaway, for the next girl to find and enjoy—left by an unknown friend.

One young girl, Morgan, described the qualities of an imaginary friend she'd had when she was younger. "For me, it was important for my imaginary friend to be someone who was kind, who was thoughtful, who stood up for herself and her friends. Someone who is responsible, and who will do what she's asked. Someone who's

Unknowingly, Sylvia first saw her cousin, Naomi, on the plane to her great-grandmother's birthday party. Once they officially met, they became good friends.

not perfect, but pretty good. Now when I think back on it," she continued a little ruefully, "I realize I was looking for all the things I wanted to be." Morgan went on to reflect that having an imaginary friend probably helped her through times when she felt lonely, or times when she wasn't getting along well with her real friends.

Grace explained her thoughts about imaginary friends, based on her experience as a youngster. "I didn't have an imaginary friend, but one of my good friends in kindergarten did. We used to carpool together, and the reason I know about him is that she introduced me to him! I pretended I could see him, and I guess she did the same. Whenever we'd be in the car together, she'd put him in the middle seat, and buckle his seat belt, and we'd have to be careful not to sit on him or squash him." Grace went on to consider why she thought her friend might have had an imaginary companion. "I think it could have been for two reasons. I don't think she was a particularly lonely person, but it might have been just a way to distract herself, and a way to have fun alone. And imaginary friends were a big thing on TV shows at the time, and maybe she felt that it sounded like a good thing. I remember it was often in the plot of the shows, and I kind of felt I wanted one, too—but I couldn't seem to get it right."

But it is not only very young children who may incorporate imaginary companions into their lives. I can speak from personal experience about the importance of having an imaginary friend in my own early teen years.

When I was young—maybe twelve or thirteen years old—I had an imaginary friend. I knew she wasn't real, but she was certainly a very important part of my personal experience. Her name was Sonnet Pat Morrow—and I have absolutely no idea, no recollection, of how or why that was her name. In those days, as throughout much of my life, I kept a diary, and, during those years when Sonnet was part of my consciousness, I addressed my writings to her, and my diary became a series of letters to her, in which I told her what was going on in my life, and I shared my thoughts, my concerns, and, at times, my despair, with her.

In other words, Sonnet Pat Morrow (and I always thought of her by all three names, although my diary addressed her only by her first name) served most of the deepest purposes of friendship. I was able to share with her my most private thoughts without feeling that she would judge me (although I allowed her some critical judgments, at least in my thoughts). She did not only exist as a pen pal; she was often in my mind, where I frequently imagined conversations with her, although I truly do not recall if I envisioned any responses from her.

During the years when Sonnet was a presence in my life, I often felt that the girls in my circle—my classmates—were judgmental, teasing, and occasionally hurtful. We attended a small private school, and many of us had been together from first grade through eighth. We knew each other's strengths and weaknesses, and, as will often happen in preadolescent groups, weaknesses were quickly detected and highlighted, and factions, teasing, and cliques were rampant. Although we were a close group, friendships realigned often, and I, for one, rarely felt I was part of the "in crowd."

But Sonnet Pat Morrow was always my friend, always on my side, always supportive and ready to listen. She was my constant friend when my other friendships wavered or became doubtful, and she was with me, somewhere in the back of my consciousness, throughout those difficult years. I hadn't thought of her until I began writing this book, but now I recognize the role she played in helping me feel more confident when I was very unsure of myself.

FRIENDS OF DIFFERENT AGES

Particularly when people are young, most of their friends are roughly the same age that they are. There are some pretty good reasons for this, the main one being proximity: we tend to bond with people nearby. Whether that is in a baby-and-mothers' group, a nursery school, school classes, or neighborhood playgrounds, kids tend to connect with others around their own age. They play at the same level, they communicate at the same level, and they develop interests common to their age cohort. And, as kids get older, the differences between the ages become more marked, often separating kids from those older or younger than they are. While three-year-olds tend to play the same way, three-year-olds and five-year-olds play and communicate very differently. The same goes for kids in the third grade and kids in the fifth grade; they generally have very different interests and ways to interact—and so friends tend to be of roughly the same age.

However, there are many benefits to having friends who are older or younger—sometimes very much older or younger. Sometimes those friendships develop naturally, and sometimes they are sought out. And friendships between people of different ages are *not* unusual. A recent study by researchers at Barna shows that almost 70 percent of Americans have a close friend who is either fifteen years older or younger than they are, while 25 percent say they have an older confidant. And of those who have a multigenerational friendship, 27 percent report having both older and younger friends.[3] Let's take a look at what some of those friendships teach us.

Friendships between Generations

For those who find themselves in a friendship with someone much older than they are—perhaps even someone of their grandparent's age—that friendship can yield rich and life-affirming benefits on both sides. For a young person who has a true friendship with an older person, they may find they have someone with whom they can talk about things they might not be able to talk about with their own parents or grandparents, someone who is nonjudgmental, and yet can bring a perspective of wisdom and experience to the questions and concerns of a young person. A teen can learn about the world, the past, and a very different way of life from listening to a senior; they can find themselves in conversations that open their eyes to history, conversations that bring vividness and detail to things they may have only read in history books or seen in films or on television, and an awareness of the wisdom, emotions, and thoughts that can develop over many years and many experiences.

For a senior, having a young friend not only brings a breath of fresh air and liveliness that may be missing in their daily life but also the opportunity to share their reminiscences, their knowledge, and their patience with a young person. For an older person, friendship with a teen can be an opportunity to learn about new things—whether music, pop culture, the latest in technology, or slang. For older people who have probably experienced losses and sadness in their lives, friendship with a young person can be a chance to open their heart to someone new, and to experience the joy of a new friendship. For Hattie, one New York City teenager, just such a connection flourished in her wonderful friendship with Rose, a woman old enough to be her grandmother. Hattie described how her friendship with Rose developed.

Hattie and Rose's Story

I have an extraordinary friend named Rose; she's ninety-four years old, and I'm so happy to call her my friend. I first met her because my godmother suggested that I visit Rose; she'd known Rose for years and thought she might be lonely.

I visited Rose for the first time last year. In the beginning, I was nervous about going to visit someone I didn't know, especially because no one came with me to introduce us. My godmother had been in touch with Rose, and asked her if I could visit, and she said yes, so I just went. I just showed up and rang the doorbell, feeling totally nervous about the whole thing.

But when the door opened, there was Rose—and she greeted me with a big smile and a hug, making my nerves disappear. She seemed so glad to see me, getting me to sit down near her, and she just started asking me about myself, my school, what I liked, did I play music—music is very important to her—and she seemed really interested in everything I said. And she told me a little about herself during that first visit; how she had trained as a pianist at the Juilliard School of Music, about how she'd lived so long in New York but couldn't go out much anymore, and about how she didn't have many people who came to visit. She just really made me feel glad to be there, and she was so interesting, and so lively.

Ever since then I've been going to visit her once a week, for almost two hours every Friday evening. And every time I come I've been serenaded—she's always playing the piano when I get there. And the visits aren't just sitting around talking. Rose taught me to play backgammon—and I can even beat her now, occasionally. Rose is amazing at backgammon—she can beat the computer in computer backgammon. She's a fierce Democrat and sometimes talks to me about politics, and about how things were in the past. Because of her age, she got a special birthday card from President Obama, and it's her prized possession. She also plays Ping-Pong, and she's a terrific cook. I thought I didn't like split pea soup until I tasted Rose's, which now I love. I don't usually eat the school lunch, but there's always something to eat at Rose's when I get there. She once made a ricotta cheesecake, which was incredible. So we end up sitting at the table a lot, having something to eat, and talking, talking, talking. In a way, I can talk to Rose about all sorts of things, even things I don't talk with my friends about, or my parents, and she always seems to have something sensible to say. Sometimes she's even calmed me down when I've been upset about something.

I've even introduced my best friend Anna to Rose. Anna was nervous about meeting a new person, especially an older person, since she had no experience with older people. But it was great— Rose put her at ease right away. And a bunch of other girls in my class want to meet Rose, because I've talked so much about her. I just find her amazing; she is so kind, so caring. And she's so interesting because she's fascinated by so many topics.

I feel like we became real friends very quickly. But I also feel that our friendship has naturally also become nurturing. I worry about Rose; in December she was hospitalized for a few days, and in May she had a stroke. She's back home now, but it makes me wonder about how much longer I'll have Rose in my life, and it makes me sad to think about, but also much more anxious to spend

At her godmother's suggestion, teenage Hattie visited ninety-four-year-old Rose. They bonded over shared interests, and Hattie eventually brought her best friend to meet Rose.

time with her, and to help her in any way I can. She's a genuine original, and I just feel so lucky to know her.

* * *

Occasionally, a friendship can lead to unexpected connections with an adult. Sylvia described her unusual experience: "I have a kind of strange situation; one of my closest friends' father is the Rabbi at my synagogue, and my parents are friends with him, so I've known him forever. And that makes things somewhat awkward sometimes. For example, when I'm visiting my friend, we often play Dungeons and Dragons. When we play, my friend's father is the Dungeon Master, and it's easy to forget that he's the Rabbi! We're just all totally into the game, and it's intense, and we have a great time together. But when we're playing, I don't even know whether I am supposed to call him Rabbi, or do I call him by his last name, or by his first name? And that feels really weird."

Speaking for myself—an older person!—I can honestly say that the friendships I have with teens—some of them friendships I've made through interviewing young people for books like this—have given me enormous pleasure. I've learned about technology I've been reluctant to deal with (Snapchat! TikTok!), music I wouldn't otherwise hear, and how different some modern-day relationships are to those of my youth. And I love hearing from younger people about what they're up to, what they're thinking, what's important to them. It keeps me energized, and feeling in touch. As one dear older friend of mine told me many years ago, "If you want to stay young, have younger friends."

Friendships with Older and Younger Kids

There are benefits to having friendships with kids a few years older or younger than you, too. Being a friend to a younger kid gives you the opportunity to be a role model, to help a younger kid navigate some of the challenges you have already mastered. Being friends with a teen or young adult a few years older than you gives you the chance to sample their experience, learn from what they know, and hear about what may be in store for you a few years down the line. Henry described to me the value he has found in having some friends a few years older than him. "I have some friends who are a year or two older than me. I got to know them a few years ago when we all were going to after-school classes together and would ride the same bus. It's great because they've got different interests from the kids in my grade, and so I learn things from them. And also, there's the cool factor; they're kind of cool, and they know that other people think they're cool, and they take advantage of that, and because other people see me with them, they think I'm cool, too. Which I'm not, really, but it works for me."

Henry continued, "They're not the only older friends I have. I feel like one of my best friends is this girl, Rayna. Rayna started out years ago as my babysitter, and in a way she's best friends with my whole family. She's out of college now, but we still stay in close touch—I even have her picture right here. I FaceTime with her a lot. She's given me a lot of advice about things I should think about for college, and told me a lot about what going away to school was like. Sometimes I even talk with her about relationships, because I feel like I can talk to her because there's the age difference, and I don't feel like she's always judging me. She's just really great, and really feels like a good friend, even though we're years apart."

Sometimes circumstances determine how friendships develop between kids of different ages. In Sylvia's case, skipping a grade in elementary school, making her a year or more younger than the other kids in her class, meant that her friendships developed with older kids. "Most of my friends are older than me because I skipped a grade, and I ended up always being the youngest in my classes. But that age difference doesn't seem to matter so much. In fact, my best friend at school this year is three or four years older than me, and a guy. My whole group of friends are a couple of years older than me, but we're friends because we like the same things, are interested in the same things. And, I'd say, we're basically at the same level of maturity, so we're not really that different."

Friendships with older teens or young adults can also provide opportunities for mentoring relationships. For instance, Tali found a warm friendship with a college student who was her mentor when she joined a local youth organization. "There are these people who are in charge of recruitment for the organization, and they're older kids, usually seniors in high school. But when I joined, there was this one girl who'd been with the organization since she started high school, and she was now in college. She's really nice, and she kind of took me under her wing when I joined, and then when we had group meetings, we just found we had a similar sense of humor, and we kind of bonded over that. She's been really helpful, especially with things like talking about college. We text a lot, and I feel like I can talk to her about a lot of things I might not want to talk to my regular girlfriends about, because she's older."

FRIENDS OF DIFFERENT GENDERS

For many reasons, most close friendships seem to be among people of the same gender. But that does not need to be the case, and sometimes friendships between the genders are deeply meaningful and close. As Kate told me, "I have one particular friend who's a boy, and we've been close friends for a long time. My friendship with him has made me understand something about friendship, and that's that boys and girls can really benefit from having a friend of a different gender. They both benefit, because they both bring a lot of different things to the table. I think that as a female, you can talk a lot with your girlfriends about emotions; maybe you don't do that so much with guys, but you can get a different perspective on things from guys. For instance, if you go to your friends for advice, you may get a different perspective from a guy friend, because guys and girls think differently sometimes. And I've found it can be nice to go to one of my close girlfriends for advice, and then to the guy who's been my friend for a long time, and hear the different advice they give me."

Kate continued: "Obviously, there's a difference between my friends who are girls and my friend who's a boy. But actually, he's quite emotional, quite feminine sometimes, maybe in a way I wouldn't expect. He obviously has boys' interests, and boys' issues; and there are things that are kind of funny to watch, to explain to him, as a female. For example, I've noticed that when we watch shows together, he has very different perspectives on the characters, based on the fact that we're different genders, and I guess we see things differently. I honestly think it's kind of a fun thing to find out how you see things from different perspectives."

Between the genders, friendships can be colored by romantic feeling—or even the consideration that romance might enter, or impact, the relationship. And for some young people, that consideration can cause anxiety. For Hattie, that was certainly something on her mind. "I know a lot of girls my age who are getting fixated on the subject of romantic relationships and dating. And I've found that if they think you have a guy friend, they assume you're dating him—which for me doesn't have to be the case. I have some friends who are guys, and it just feels easy to be friends with them, especially because we have some interests in common. But I can understand why some girls think it has to be romantic—they can't imagine just being friends. But I want to keep things separate. For example, I have some guy friends who I think of as my tennis friends; we have a great time on the tennis court, and we sometimes hang out together in a group. One of the guys asked me out on a date, but I said no. I found it stressful, because I want to keep those friendships as friendships; I don't want to have them get romantic; I don't want to mix friendship with dating."

Sara reflected on how having friends of another gender has changed for her over the years. "There was a boy who was in elementary school with me, and I think we've been good friends since fifth grade, at an age when it was weird for boys and girls to be friends. He wasn't friends with a lot of the boys in our grade, and I think that the girls—even my close friends—felt that we had to pretend we were not friends with him, so that other people would not make fun of *us* for being friends with him. And now that's not true at all! Maybe because we're all a little bit older, but people in my grade are *for sure* friends with boys—now, if you're not friends with boys, it's considered weird. So it's like it keeps changing, and I have to keep up!"

Being comfortable with friends of another gender varies with age. As Emily put it, "Last year, when we were mostly twelve and thirteen, was really the first year where anyone would even mention being friends with boys. And mostly it was some girls in our grade who thought it was cool to be friends with boys, but it turns out that they weren't actually friends with them because they *wanted* to be friends; they just wanted to be cool. But in my group of friends, we were all different genders, and those were really good friendships; we'd always sit together at lunch, we talked a lot about everything, we laughed a lot, and we really cared about each other. I think that was pretty unusual in our grade, when mostly kids stuck with friends of the same gender."

Henry agreed. "Friends with girls and boys? That has changed over the years. But it genuinely changed when I got past middle school. In middle school, a lot of the girls didn't seem to like me, I don't know why, so I didn't have friends who were girls until more recently. Now I have a lot of guy friends, but I also have some friends who are girls; I definitely have more in common with the guys, but some of the girls are interested in the same things I am, even though they have a lot of different interests, too."

Emily put it even more bluntly: "I think everyone should just be friends with whomever they want; if it's a boy, great; if it's a girl, great. Whatever! Don't let social pressure get to you."

As young teens, kids often find themselves in group friendships of mixed genders that grow up around common interests. As Tali explained, "Before the pandemic quarantines, my friend Aden, with some of our other friends—boys and girls—would try to get together every week, watching all the Marvel movies. We were planning to watch *Black Widow* together, but then coronavirus happened, so we're somewhat behind; but we're all kind of close, and we really bonded over loving the Marvel movies." Tali continued, "In my class, everyone is kind of friends; even the girls who are not in my group seem to be comfortable having friends who are boys."

GROUP FRIENDSHIPS

For many young people, at some point in their lives their most important friendships are group friendships. Sometimes, especially for adolescents, being in a group is more comfortable than pairing off. As Kate put it, "There are four of us who are really good friends; we kind of have a very tight-knit group. It's not an exclusive thing; we each have other friends, too, but we mostly just kind of stay together. I maybe bounce around among other friends more than the others do, but generally the four of us stick together in our little group. I think that may be because the other girls are actually a little bit shy, and feel more comfortable within the group."

Sylvia gave her personal rationale: "All my friends are pretty much in the same group. It just feels comfortable for me that way. If I'm with my group, I feel like the responsibility for socializing is not just on me. And especially now, during Covid, when everything's online, I can introduce my friends to my cousin, for example, and I won't feel that having to introduce her is going to be that weird, like it would be if I had to do it in person, because I can just add her to the group chat. Whereas, if we were in person, it would be super awkward, because I'm not great at socializing in person, and doing things like making introductions."

SHORT-TERM OR TEMPORARY FRIENDSHIPS

We generally think of friendships as being long lasting; after all, we put a lot of energy and emotion into friendships, and we hope and expect that friendships will endure. But there are some circumstances where friendships are brief, or temporary; not because of any ill will or breakup, but because they are, of necessity, time limited. Those friendships, though, do not necessarily have less value or meaning than long-term friendships. Often they can be meaningful, and even life changing, and yet the friendship itself is brief.

Hattie says she's had lots of short-term friendships—mostly, she says, "sort of summer friends," whether from the beach club, or sailing and tennis classes; these friendships didn't last once Hattie got back to the school year. "We didn't correspond, and I basically didn't feel the need to reach out to continue the friendships." She did find, though, that during the month she spent at an academic program in Cambridge, England, "It was good to have new friends. At the program, we had to eat dinner with someone each night, and I became friendly with this one guy and we have stayed in touch since then. I found that in a temporary situation like that, where you know you're only going to be in it for a brief time, you can make what I think of as 'good-enough friends'; they're your friends when you need them, but when you move on, there are no hard feelings because everyone is in the same boat."

Tali has returned to the same summer camp for several years in a row and has developed friendships with girls she met there, but, she says, "I'm friends with them at camp, but then after camp, I don't really talk to them. I may think about them; for instance, right here I have a picture from camp this summer, and I always look at it, and it reminds me that camp was fun. I text with some of the people a lot. When we go back to camp, we're friends again—but during the year, we're not so close. It's weird, but in camp, we can become really close, and then, during the year, you have other friends, and you don't really think about the camp friends, no matter how close you were with them in the summer. Then if you see them again the next year, you'll immediately feel that same closeness—it revives somehow. It's like a plant, or a garden; it can have dry spells, but when it gets watered, it blooms again."

For Jimmy, such camp friendships created some mixed emotions. "I feel that camp friendships are temporary friendships. There's no one I'm friendly with at my school who goes to my camp. So it's like camp is a whole separate bunch of friends. And even though I have friends at camp, I don't think I'm as close to them as I am with my school friends because I haven't known them as long, or I don't see them as much. Even if I see the camp friends for seven or eight weeks in the summer, once I leave camp, I don't see them during the year, and maybe don't even think about them. And if you go back the next year and you see them again, a whole year has passed, so that the stuff that happened the year before is probably forgotten, or you kind of got over it. And you can kind of start over again.

"In a way, it feels like things at camp don't matter as much as they do in my regular life. Whatever happens during the summer, once you get home, no one will know the difference—like it's not real life. In a way, I wish that my school friends would be at camp with me so that we could share the same experiences; but on the other hand, it's good that we're not together, because then camp is a different world for me, with a whole bunch of other people, and all the baggage you may have picked up in camp just goes away after the summer."

Max described his experience with a brief, vacation friendship. "My whole family went for a family vacation at this big resort place. I didn't have a whole lot to do and was kind of wandering around on the second day we got there. There was this other kid, whose whole family was also there, and I saw them playing Frisbee, and asked if I could join, and that was fun and kind of got us started. And then the next day it was raining, and I saw him walking down the corridor, and we started playing with some stuff we found around, making up some crazy game, and we ended up cracking each other up in laughter. And then, for the whole week or so we were there, we'd meet up and do things together, play ball outside, Frisbee, hang around. And it felt like we were friends, but just for that week while we were both there. After we left, I didn't see him again. We exchanged email addresses, but then I lost his email, so we just lost touch. We had a great time while we were there, and it felt like we were friends, but I never really thought about him again until now."

Sara also found that keeping in touch with temporary friends wasn't easy. "I went to sleepaway camp for two years, and I also went to day camp for a while, even this summer, during the pandemic. I found that even though I make good friends in camp, I'm *not* good at reaching out after the summer, keeping track of emails and stuff. With some of those summer friends, I wish I had, because they were so nice. I think about how I might see them next summer, especially the ones from when I was younger who I really liked a lot. But I realize that I didn't understand then that I should take their phone number, which now I wish I had done, because they were really nice, and I think we could have been good friends."

Sometimes the temporariness of such short-term friendships can be bittersweet. As Grace put it, "I think it's a little disappointing, especially if you're on vacation, to realize that someone you got friendly with will probably disappear from your life. Like, 'Oh great, we had a wonderful week together, but now I'll probably never see you again.' And that's happened to me, because the girl I became friendly with one time when I was on vacation lives all the way on the other side of the country. So I did feel kind of bad about that. At least with camp friends—and I'd say I have one or two who I don't really stay in touch with outside of camp—I always think how it will be nice to go back to camp and see them again and say, 'Oh, I've missed you so much, I haven't talked to you in so long!' and catch up. And then it feels like you've kept them as friends all along."

Emily's camp friendships echoed the experience of many young people. "I went to sleepaway camp for two summers," Emily explained, "and a lot of the people I met—not everyone, but most of the people—I lost touch with after camp was over. But we were such good friends during the summer. I think that definitely is something that camp does; it creates these intense, really close friendships for a few weeks, or a month or two, and then, unless you really work to stay in touch, they dissolve. Maybe you'll see them the following summer, maybe not. And then they just sort of fade from your mind, except for the occasional memory, or seeing a picture from camp, something like that. Sometimes it's that way at school, too," Emily went on. "At school, I had a few friends who were in my class, and we were good friends for a few months, or even just for a few weeks, and I don't know, maybe because we weren't in the same class the next year, or we weren't in the same friend group, we weren't friends anymore. Not that we fought, or anything like that, but we just kind of moved on."

LONG-DISTANCE FRIENDSHIPS

Online Friendships

A relatively new phenomenon, developed over the last twenty or so years, is online friendship. The closest thing to that in prior years might have been having a pen pal or correspondence friendship; in both cases, these relationships usually begin without ever having met someone face to face. Such a relationship may proceed to in-person friendship, but often it never gets to that point. A primary difference between these relationships is that because of the amplified possibility for online connections to be fraudulent or dishonest, with fabricated identities and mischievous or even criminal intent behind some interactions, there is much more potential for harm than there was in previous years.

Many young people are aware of the dangers and try to take sensible precautions to prevent becoming enmeshed in dangerous communications and interactions. Unfortunately, young people are sometimes not able to judge—or are in denial about—suspicious or dangerous elements in social media connections. While at some points parents or adults can control or supervise access to online interactions, that is not always the case; therefore, it is extremely important to understand and respect the potential for harm in corresponding online. It is not my goal here to explain how to safely navigate the Internet, but I think it's important to acknowledge and consider the risks involved in communicating with strangers while online.

For many teenagers, the word *friend* may mean an "in-person" friend or an "online" friend, and to some kids, those friendships may seem similar, if not the same. There can certainly be benefits to both types of relationship. But while a person can develop a close online friendship with someone they have never met in person, an in-person friendship brings with it a very special dynamic almost impossible to match online. Maria Konnikova, a writer and psychologist, described the important element that bonds a face-to-face friendship as "the nature of shared experience: you laugh together; you dance together; you gape at the hot-dog eaters on Coney Island together." She continues, "We do have a social-media equivalent—sharing, liking, knowing that all of your friends have looked at the same cat video on YouTube as you did—but it lacks the synchronieity of shared experience."[4] For many people, teenager or adult, nothing can replicate the warmth, the immediacy, and the deep connection we feel when we are actually in the presence of good friends.

That said, there can also be tremendous benefit from online friendships, and the relationships that can be forged between young people while online can be wonderful. With this incredible technology, young people can connect with others outside of their communities, and even around the world. Because of the ease of finding others with common interests, the process of making friends online is almost effortless. Therefore, even—or especially—young people who find it difficult to meet people in person, whether because of shyness or practical impediments to meeting "in real life," can find it easy to forge acquaintanceships online that turn into genuine friendships.

For many kids, the gateway to making Internet friendships is through online gaming. Because you are connecting with others who share your interests, it's an easy environment in which to find people who might become friends. As Ben, who grew up going to school in Great Britain, explained, "I don't have that many close online friends, since most of my good friends are in-person friends. But you can certainly get friendly in the online world; it's easy, especially for people who don't have friends, to find compatible people in the gaming world."

Social media, certainly, is an almost universal way to connect with others, but it does raise issues that concern some kids. Henry shared some of his thoughts and concerns about different types of online friendships. "There's a difference between actually meeting someone online, or just following them on their social media or YouTube account, and you have to be cautious. If you actually meet someone online, if they actually try to talk to you, unless you truly think they're trustworthy, don't talk to them, or block them. On

YouTube, sometimes you'll have subscribers who try to chat with you. For instance, I have a small YouTube channel, and I have a few subscribers who I know in person, but sometimes other people try to chat with me, and I know you have to be careful."

I asked one young woman, Sylvia, whether she'd ever met in person anyone she'd become friends with online. "No, I've still not done that. This one girl I met online, I'd feel very comfortable meeting her in person, because I know for a fact she's my age, and a real person. But it would be hard, because she lives in Texas, and I don't know how we would be able to meet."

Grace explained some of her thoughts about online friendships. "I do have some friends who are only online friends. I'm not on Facebook, but I am on Instagram and Snapchat, and there are definitely people on Snapchat who I didn't know that well before, but then I started talking to them online, and now we're really good friends. There's this one girl who I've met once or twice; and we FaceTimed once after that. But I don't really like having online friends whom I haven't met in person. It's a little uncomfortable, for me at least; I don't like that I've never gotten to meet them in person. I haven't gotten to feel them out. I haven't gotten to know whether they're the same in person as they are online; it just makes me a little bit uncomfortable. So until I meet someone in person, if I'm talking with them online, I might be a little bit more reserved, in general, kind of closed off; not cold, but just a little bit more private. And I think that's important, because you're sharing your information with someone who's almost a stranger; so I don't like to get into personal stuff too much until I've met them in person."

Grace continued, "Some of my friends have had online friends whom they've never met, and it's worries me: for instance, how do you even know if she's a girl, like she says? What if it's just some random guy, some weirdo? And I've always been a little freaked out by that. When I asked one of my friends about whether she was sure the person she was online with was a girl, she told me, 'Of course! I have pictures!,' and I said, 'How do you know they're her?' And my friend said, 'Well, I trust her.' So I told her, 'Okay, you trust her, but don't give out your social security number!' That's been drilled into me by my parents a lot, a little bit more, I guess, than some other kids. I think it's a very generational thing. A lot of my friends, actually most of my friends, have friends on Snapchat who they've never met, but they talk with a lot. I talk with my friends on Snapchat, but if I haven't met you, I'm not talking that much. The thing about online friends is just that it's always seemed a little bit risky for me."

Emily, on the other hand, regrets not having the opportunity to make online friends. "My sister and I do not do Snapchat, Instagram, those kinds of things. Our parents do not want us to be on social media. But honestly, especially now, I do want to get Instagram—I wouldn't post on it, but in my grade, so many people talk about Instagram. I don't think I would even want to post, but I do want to know what they're talking about, and be part of the conversation. But as of now, we are not on it, and that makes me feel kind of left out."

Pen Pals or Correspondence Friendships

These days, many young people have friendships with other kids they meet online. But in the days before the Internet—and still, even today—many young people developed friendships through corresponding with each other—popularly described as pen pals. Sometimes having a pen pal originates as a school assignment so that young people can practice written social skills, communication skills, handwriting (in the days before computers and even today), spelling, vocabulary, or even a foreign language. Sometimes a parent suggests that a young person write to a cousin or the youngster of one of their acquaintances. And sometimes finding a pen pal is something young people themselves are motivated to do, whether just for fun or to find out about another culture or country by writing to someone abroad, or to practice writing in a another language. But while very often such a remote connection does not continue long, occasionally pen pals become true friends, and sometimes a relationship developed through the written word flourishes over long periods of time, whether or not the two people involved ever meet each other in person.

Tali told me about her experience with a pen pal. "I have a friend named Jack; we got to know each other because my dad worked with his dad. I don't remember this, but my mom tells me this one story all the time, how one time our two families were on a plane together when Jack and I were tiny. My mom says Jack and I sat in the same seat and watched a movie together for the whole flight and had a great time together. Well, when I was in elementary school, we had an assignment to write to a pen pal, and I wrote to Jack, who was living in China at the time. It was when everyone was sending around Flat Stanley cutouts of a character from the book *Flat Stanley*,[5] so I made a Flat Tali, and we sent it to Jack in China, and he took a picture of himself with Flat Tali in front of the house where he lived. It was my choice to write to Jack, and we kept in touch for quite a while after that, writing back and forth. My dad's still in touch with his dad, and I know they've moved back to the United States, so I hope that after the pandemic we'll be able to get together again."

Sara's experience with having a correspondence—or communication—friendship was a little different. As with many kids, it originated as a school program, and she didn't personally know the student she was communicating with before the program. "In school, when we had computer class, our teacher tried to connect us with a school in India, so that we could communicate with students there and learn more about our differences and similarities. The program lasted for only a short time, a couple of weeks, and then it stopped because of technological problems. We were trying to communicate on a Smart Board, but we couldn't really hear each other very well. I had actually started to make a connection with this one girl, but then we weren't able to continue when things got a bit chaotic. I was really interested in learning more about her, and how things were where she lived, so I felt a little sad about that."

As with short-term or temporary friends, it's often hard to keep a friendship going with correspondence friendships. When Emily was assigned a pen pal in Israel when she was in elementary school, her relationship was able to grow beyond the initial assignment. As she says, "Once a week we would write letters to each other, and as the year went by, we got to know more and more about each other, and how some things were the same for us, and how some things were different. After the year ended, we gave each other our phone numbers, and exchanged email addresses, and then for the next year, we actually would email a lot, and text a lot, and it felt like we were friends. But then over the past few months, I haven't really talked to her—she emailed me once, I emailed back—but it's complicated, because she lives in Israel, and with the time difference and all, it's been hard. We had been texting a lot, but then, it kind of faded out. It's like with camp friends; right after camp, I'm still very close with them electronically, but then a few months later, you kind of tend to forget."

With all these relationships, and any other form that friendship might take, it's important to understand that friendship is not a static thing; friendships, no matter what type, may grow or fade; they may progress from a casual acquaintanceship to a deep, personal, long-term friendship—and sometimes even reverse that progress. Cousins who were close friends in childhood may revert to "just" being cousins. Pen pals or online friends may meet and form close in-person bonds. And short-term friendships may revive years later and pick up where they left off. But whatever the "type" of friendship, it is sure to bring pleasure and value to your life through sharing the experience.

Part Two

Expectations and Challenges

4

HOW DO FRIENDSHIPS HAPPEN?

Friendships develop in all sorts of ways. Sometimes it seems almost instantaneous, when you happen to meet someone and you just "click," and other times you find that you've known someone casually for a long time, and almost without knowing how, they've become a close friend. Some people seem to find making friends almost effortless; they meet someone, they talk with them, and before very much time passes, they feel like they're kindred spirits and really good friends. Other people find it intimidating even to contemplate becoming friends with someone and may not be able to imagine getting into a conversation, let alone a friendship, with someone they don't know.

For many kids, friendships happen because their parents are friends with other parents. Tali recalled that she's known her earliest friend, Sofia, "literally since before I can remember. We lived in the same neighborhood, and our parents met each other and became friends. Sofia and I instantly became friends, too, and we've been best friends ever since." I heard from many of the young people I interviewed that their earliest friends were children whose mothers met during pregnancy or in "mommy and me" groups. When two mothers, or a group of mothers, become friends, and the babies play together while the mothers chat, friendships happen naturally, and very often continue for many years.

For Jordana, that was the way she met one of her closest friends. "I have a friend who I only know because her mom and my mom are good friends from before I was even born. She lives in California now, but we met when we were really little and she lived in New Jersey and we stayed at her house. After she moved to California, we took a trip to stay with her again, and that's when we got really close. She has an older brother, and he was nice, but a bit distant, and besides, I don't usually hang out with kids who are older than me. So I spent a lot of time with her during that visit, and I really felt a better connection with her, and we're still very close."

On occasion, parents don't even have to be friends to foster a friendship between their kids. Max described how he got to know his best friend many years ago. "One time, when we were little kids, and both at our community center, we were both hanging out in the kids' section near the gym. Our mothers were in the same exercise class, but they didn't know each other. That day, when they came out of class, they saw that we had started playing together and seemed to be having a good time. So they asked for each other's phone numbers, and it was our mothers who got us together for a playdate. I don't know how many years ago that was, but we've been great friends ever since."

Certainly, many friendships start as school friendships. Sylvia described how one of her best friendships grew from a school meeting, even though it had a rather unprepossessing start. "My best friend ever in school started talking to me on a field trip. I'd known her a little from before, but when I first met her I really didn't like her. She and some other kids were always talking about this video game that I don't play, and she was pretty obsessed with the game. And then she started talking to me on this field trip, and I kind of liked her, and she joined our friend group. But then they seemed to always be talking about the video game, and I felt super left out and started to get pretty fed up with her. But then the next year, they all stopped talking about the game so much, and she and I became best friends. When we were in school together, we didn't have a lot of time to talk or do things, but when we were able to be together on weekends, we would sit around, talk, play video games. Sometimes we cook together, or bake things."

Many young people today find friends, and communities of friends, online, whether on social media or game platforms. Sylvia explained how that worked for her: "It's a lot about cultural interests. I play *Minecraft*, and so I'm on one server for people who play *Minecraft*. And I'm on another server for people who like the movie *The Old Guard*, and then I've met people through a wiki for comics. And I met my friend Claire through this wiki for people who like books by Rainbow Rowell, which I'm really into." While Sylvia has not met any of these online friends in person, she does feel that their friendship develops through texting back and forth and talking about their common areas of interest.

There is much concern these days about the potential for young people to be scammed by Internet predators, who hide behind online personas, pretending to be a teenager and connecting with unsuspecting young people, with potentially devastating results. I asked Sylvia about what precautions she takes with online friends, and whether she had any concerns about these Internet friendships. Answering, she explained further about her experience with Claire: "I've talked with her on FaceTime, so I actually saw her, and from that I know that there's literally no way she can be anything but my age. I'm also *very* careful. Claire doesn't know my last name. She doesn't know any of my personal information. Also, Discord, the server we use, is primarily for young people, so I think there is less to worry about, like whether you might be texting with some creepy old person. And also, if I want to direct-message someone, I am *very* careful about what I say. I never post something where everyone can see it; I have private conversations with my friends."

One of the most challenging experiences anyone—adult or youth—can face is moving to another home, another community, an entirely new environment. Particularly for young people, having to move from one community to a very different one—and having to make new friends in a very different environment—poses all sorts of emotional and practical complications and is often a very stressful, anxious time. Kate, a seventeen-year-old who now lives in Upstate New York, talked with me about her experience with just such a transition. In her case, Kate moved from a quiet suburban development on Long Island to a much more urban environment in a city close to the Canadian border, but her experience having to make new friends could take place anywhere.

KATE'S STORY

When I was about thirteen or fourteen years old, my family moved from the neighborhood where I'd grown up to a completely different place, a different kind of community. We moved from a small town in Long Island to Buffalo the summer before I went into eighth grade. It was a really hard time for me; the two places are very different environments, and it was happening at such a difficult time during adolescence. It felt like one day I was in the center of a whole circle of friends on Long Island, and then I wasn't. That was really hard, especially at first. Because as far as making friends went, I had to start, basically, from scratch.

When we moved to Buffalo, it was kind of hard for me to figure out where I fit in. I suddenly found that I had to be the one reaching out to people, and I actually went from being really introverted and shy to being an extrovert. I'm not sure what made me decide that, but for a while, I decided it had to be "Fake it till you make it" and just go way out of my comfort zone to meet people and try to make friends.

And eventually I did find people. At first I thought I might meet kids in the neighborhood, but it turned out that there weren't kids my age close by; there were mostly older people or families with younger kids. My brother found kids, but he's a lot younger than me, and it was the kind of place where he made friends with the neighbors' kids very quickly. He was about nine years old, and younger kids, when they see another kid around their age, just seem to be able to go over and say hello, and then, "Let's play ball," and next thing you know they're friends. But I wasn't finding anyone my age in the neighborhood.

So, when school started, I signed up to join a bunch of clubs and sports teams. And that's how I met my best friend, through lacrosse. I'd seen her in school, and then when we both went out for lacrosse, we became close friends very quickly, probably because we immediately had an interest in common. And that's how I made other friends, too, mostly through clubs and teams. I have a whole circle now, and in a way, it seems like I've always known them. But in the beginning, before I made friends, I was really feeling lost.

I think what was important was that I started to realize that it's hard for a lot of people to meet new people and to make friends. And you have to stop overthinking and worrying so much about, "What if I say something wrong? What if I do the wrong thing?" You have to calm yourself down and realize that the person you're talking to is probably feeling the same awkward tension you are. There may be some people who don't feel awkward about meeting new people, but I think most people do, and I think it helps a lot to remember that. And it's important to remember that even people you don't know have feelings, and if you're self-conscious about talking to them, you have to remember that they probably feel the same things you do, and think the same things you do, at least most of the time. Especially with teenagers, most of us are in the same boat right now; we all feel the same way with the whole Covid thing, and all the crazy stuff that's going on. So we all have things in common, and at least that's a start to getting to know someone. I think it's also helpful to always have some kind of conversation starter in your head; something that you can ask pretty much anyone, just to have an opening to start a conversation. One thing that I've found is that if you're trying to find something in common to talk about with someone, if you can find a TV show that you both like, that's a really good one to go off on.

* * *

For some young people, although they are able to make friends, they don't seem to know how they actually do it. To those kids, it seems as though they "fall" into friendships rather than actively seeking them or working to make them happen. For example, when

After moving to a new city, Kate joined clubs and sports teams to make new friends.

I asked Judith, a young woman in California, how she made friends, she answered adamantly, "I have *no* idea. I'm terrible at it." But then, she continued, "I generally make friends by either being on an online server and being in a conversation online, or by my friends introducing me to their friends." Those are certainly not uncommon ways friendships happen, but some kids seem to feel that "making friends" requires more active intent.

And there *are* ways to pursue friendship more actively, without coming on as pushy, or as if you are trying to force a friendship. As Emma Pattee wrote in an article in the *New York Times* a few years ago, "If you want closer friendships, the first step is to decide you're going to do something about it." Quoting Sue Johnson, a psychologist who studies bonding and attachment, Pattee continues, "We think about relationships as things that happen to us, but the truth is that we make them happen."[1] Putting yourself in situations where there are other kids whom you might find congenial—with interests you might have in common, and similar values and goals—is one good way to find friends in a natural way. Joining a club or interest group, going out for a team—whether it's sports, debating, math, or science—puts you into a group more or less your own age, and with your interests. If you have a religious community, consider joining a youth group or choir. In your neighborhood community, think about volunteering to help when there are events or activities that can use some extra hands. By participating in activities where everyone present is working together on a shared goal, you will find yourself talking with people informally about whatever activity you're doing. That kind of shared experience is often a good starting point for friendships to develop.

For many kids, a large amount of their social interaction comes at lunchtime. For kids who eat lunch in a school cafeteria, the dynamics of who sits with whom, which tables the "cool" kids corral, and where the loners sit can become fraught with anxiety and social awkwardness. And when kids are allowed off the school campus for lunch, those divisions can become even more obvious. As Lydia Denworth writes in her book *Friendship*, "No wonder lunch looms large. . . . It is why the movies are filled with so many scenes of anxious children holding a tray and not knowing where to sit."[2] But the cafeteria, and the lunchtime routine, can also be a way to find friends and solidify friendships. Sitting next to someone at lunch, whether you are alone together or part of a group, is a stage for conversation—even if it is just about what you are eating.

In an article in *Psychology Today*, author Karen Karbo explores what attracts and binds people to each other as friends.[3] As she describes, one particular factor that helps move two people from acquaintanceship to friendship is self-disclosure, or reciprocity. Being able to open up to someone, and have them open up to you, is one of the first steps to the intimacy of true friendship. Other important elements in cementing a solid friendship are trust and emotional generosity—being able to be there for the other person; as she writes, "If anything, it's giving and not receiving that makes us value a friend more."

Spending time with someone is another—maybe the most—important factor in enabling a friendship to happen. The more time you spend with someone, the better you get to know them—and the way you find out if you *want* to spend more time with them. Granted, during the restrictions of the pandemic, spending time with someone became harder, if not impossible, to do. And the give and take of a close in-person friendship builds an intimacy that is harder to form through electronic technology. But from what I've heard from young people I interviewed for this book, good friendships were formed, and true friendships solidified, by spending quality time together on calls, texting, video chats, and other electronic platforms.

In my conversations with young people about how they thought friendships happen, I heard the same words and phrases repeated: to be a friend, someone had to be trustworthy, had to listen, had to share thoughts and feelings, as well as have common interests. They looked for people they could depend on being there for them, to "have their back," to be funny and kind. However they initially met their friends, these were the common elements that drew them to someone, and that led them into friendship. And these steps to making friends remain the same, whether in person or online: spending time together; sharing personal feelings and thoughts, allowing intimacy to grow; being honest and open with each other; being reliable; and showing willingness to be a generous and sensitive listener are the basic steps anyone can take toward making a friendship happen.

5

HOW DO YOU RECOGNIZE
A TRUE FRIEND?

"It's hard to tease out what friendship is, why a friend is different from anybody else in the world. What is it about that person that, in your head or your heart, makes you know they're your friend?"—Sylvia, age fourteen

Most people tend to have many friends, but these friendships differ in their levels of closeness. Sometimes these relationships may be as superficial and occasional as an acquaintanceship; other times they are indeed friendships, but never blossom into the kind of long-term, close relationships that take on a deep meaning in a person's life. Some friendships become very strong bonds between people, often lasting over long periods of time—even lifetimes. Strong friendships can endure, despite challenges of distance or other outside forces. What is it that makes some people become "best friends"? What makes some friendships deepen beyond the ordinary, and what makes one recognize a "true friend"?

When I asked young people why they feel that some friends become "best friends," they had remarkably similar insights. Jordana, a young woman in New York, explained that, "with a best friend, I feel different things for them than I do with regular friends. I feel like I have a better time with them, or know them better. With regular friends, you might know them, and enjoy hanging out with them, but a best friend is like your sister." For Cipi, "I think it's the quality of the time, versus the time of the time—it doesn't matter how much time you spend together, it's that the time you spend with your best friend is just better than with a regular friend. With a 'just friend,' I might share an interest with them, or they're someone I can occasionally talk to. But Jordi, my best friend, is an awesome friend; I can share everything with her. A regular friend might not always have your back; for instance, if someone was bullying you, a regular friend might not be willing to risk themselves to defend you, but I feel that my best friend would do that for me." And as Ben put it, "If you are thinking to yourself, is this person my friend? Are they the right person to be friends with? You can usually judge by how the person acts, how the person looks at you, how they act around you. If you notice that they act one way with others, but they seem to become easier and more relaxed around you, it probably means they truly enjoy your company. And that's a real friend."

When Grace, a young woman in Pennsylvania, told me about her best friend, who now lives across the country from her, she spoke about why their friendship endured despite the difficulty of trying to stay in touch, considering the time difference and difference in schedules. Thinking about it, she explained those difficulties away, saying simply, "I think she's just one of those people it's easy to stay in touch with. Because you always want to talk with her—at least I do."

As Judith, who lives on the outskirts of Los Angeles, told me, "I'm closer with my best friend than I am with just my regular friends. I think I'm closer with her because I've known her for a very long time, and we see eye to eye on stuff, and have lots in common, and like doing the same thing. We both love playing with dogs, and mainly just doing stuff with animals. I met her in kindergarten, but it was not until second grade that we really became friends. And then I think it was in third grade that we became best friends. I think what distinguishes a best friend is that you know your best friend better than most of your other friends. Maybe you are more alike with your best friend than with other people, and that's what makes you closer than with your 'just friends.'"

When I asked young people what characteristics make a good friend, I heard the same words echoed many times. Those words were *kindness*, *loyalty*, *trust*, *humor*, and *honesty*, as well as *interests in common*. Morgan, for instance, says her friends are "kind, they are funny, and they stand up for others if someone is being bullied. And they make me laugh!" Jordi summed up the characteristics of her best friends: "All of my friends have one thing similar to each other; they're all so sweet, in their own way." For Sylvia, "the most important thing to me in a friend is having someone who you can talk to, and who is funny, and who won't get overly freaked out about little things." In Ben's words, "I think best friends have the best time together because the friendship is mutual, equal." And Emily from New York City put it well when she said, "I would say that a best friend is someone who cares about you, who *wants* to be your friend."

Sharing personal stories, knowing things about each other that you may not have told anyone else, can be an important part of friendship. And bonds of friendship are built when such sharing is mutual. As Leni, the teenage protagonist of Kristin Hannah's novel *The Great Alone*, realizes, "He had told her something personal about himself, something that mattered. She needed to do the same thing. Wasn't that how true friendship worked?"[1]

"My best friend," Emily continued, "is definitely the friend I made in second grade. Since the end of second grade, I don't think there was a day that we didn't sit together at lunch. We have been in the same class every year since, and we are extremely close; we talk to each other *all* the time. Everyone in our grade knew we were best friends because we were so close." When I asked Emily to differentiate between a best friend and an acquaintance or "regular" friend, she described the difference this way: "You spend a lot of time with your best friend, you tell them everything, and they help you. An acquaintance is someone you talk to if you need something, like homework." Another good example she gave is that "a friend is someone you might *choose* to be partners with."

Knowing each other for a long time can certainly play a large part in deepening a friendship into a best friendship. In Grace's view, "People that you're meant to be friends with will always stick with you far longer than others, and they'll always come through for you in the end." And Tali, who now lives in Maryland, expanded on that: "My closest friend relationship is with Sofia; we have been there for each other ever since we were little. We were in school together when I lived in California, which was most of my early life. There was one year, when I still lived in California, that she went to public school part of the year, but then she came back during the middle of the year to the same school we'd started at, so we were together again. We've always been there for each other, for the major milestones of life, like birthdays; it was important to us to be there for each other. She's just been in my life since before I can remember. I hadn't seen Sofia for a long time, but when I was able to visit her in California before Covid, it was like no time had passed, like we'd never been separated."

With that, Tali realized another aspect of true friendship: time and distance apart can disappear when friends are reunited. As the fictional Leni realizes later in *The Great Alone*, "He taught her something new about friendship: it picked right back up where you'd left off, as if you hadn't been apart at all."[2] Kate reflected a very similar feeling; as she put it, "I found that with my friend from back home, where I lived before we moved, when we get on the phone we talk and it's just like I left yesterday, even though we may not have talked in a month."

Sometimes, the origins of a deep friendship may be remembered slightly differently by the two parties involved, as it is with Jordana and her best friend, Cipi. The different perspectives, however, make it no less meaningful a relationship.

JORDANA AND CIPI'S STORY: BEST FRIENDS

In Jordana's recollection, it was a shirt that turned a chance meeting into a deep friendship. She recalled, "I met one of my best friends a bunch of years ago at a local park. It was funny, because the reason we met was that we were both wearing the same shirt. As soon as we noticed that, we started laughing. Then I asked her if she wanted to play with me. In those days, my father and I had this superhero game that we played together, and when I asked Cipi to play, everything just took off from there. When I think about meeting Cipi, I think about how we might still have met because we had the same shirt, but it could have turned out very differently. If she had been snooty to me when I asked her if she wanted to play with us, or had just said no, it probably would have ended there. But the way she answered me, laughing about our shirts, made it so easy. And then when she played this crazy, made-up superheroes game with us, and it turned out she knew *all* the superheroes—I couldn't believe it, it was totally amazing that we found each other. And then we picked all our favorite superhero characters, and we started making a wonderful setting for our game in the park, and that was our special spot for years. From the beginning, I felt that she was just really sweet, and really fun. And then when she kind of jumped right in and played the superheroes game with me, that was a connection I have with no one else. And we've felt that connection ever since."

Cipi remembers their meeting slightly differently, but it made just as big an impression on her as it did on Jordana. "I was in the park not far from where we live; we called it Rainbow Park because it has this climbing apparatus like a rainbow, and I was running around on the playground when I saw Jordi and her parents playing tag. I didn't have anybody to play with, and I asked if I could play tag with them; actually, it was really my dad who suggested it. I'm very friendly, but he's even more friendly, and he told me to go over and ask to play with them. So I went over, and when I asked, 'Can I play with you?,' they said, 'Sure!' And then we all started playing tag, even my dad, and we had a great time. When we finally stopped, it was my dad who said, 'Oh, we all live so close, we should get together sometime,' and by the next day, we were eating dinner together, outside, in Rainbow Park. From the first moment, it was like Jordi and me were just meant to be best friends. Soon afterwards we had our first sleepover, and then we just kept on doing it, almost every weekend. Jordi's like my soul mate; we're just like BFFs. I have other best friends, but Jordi's like the *most best*."

* * *

Close friendships develop in many ways, sometimes quickly, and sometimes over a longer period of time. Sara recounted the beginning of her friendship with the girl who became her closest friend: "I actually met my very best friend, Karen, in third grade, during lunch. I had gotten into some kind of fight with my friends, I really don't remember what it was about, but I was upset and got up to switch to another table. I decided to sit at a table where another girl was sitting—I honestly don't think I had ever seen her before, until I saw her sitting in the back of the lunchroom. And I decided to just sit down, and truthfully—this was third grade—we just became instant friends! And we didn't have such similar interests at that time, but we just kind of clicked, and we had so much to talk about, and within three days, we were best friends, pretty much. And we still are."

Time spent together certainly has the potential to create a deeper bond with someone, whether it is sharing a common interest or activity, or just spending time in the same environment. Seventeen-year-old Hattie described what friendships meant to her, and how an acquaintanceship transformed into a deeply rewarding best friendship.

Hattie told me, "I've never felt a strong need to have friends. Even as a small child, I have always been able to entertain myself and keep myself occupied, and somehow I never felt that I missed having friendships. But by the time I was in fifth grade, I'd become friends with a group of three other girls, and it was fine; they were all sort of friends with each other, but I always felt that they tended to overdramatize things and I didn't really feel comfortable with that. They had arguments over very trivial things, and I didn't really feel that their values aligned with mine; I thought of them more as just friends by association. Then there was a falling out among them, and since I wasn't really interested in being part of the drama,

I walked away from the group, and they more or less decided to all take a break from each other. When that school year ended, I was kind of relieved that the group friendship had ended. I just thought of it as a good learning experience.

"But then I started to worry over the summer, because I would be starting middle school, and I was afraid that I wouldn't have any friends. I didn't know how the year was going to turn out, and I didn't know whether there would be problems with the other girls from that group. But the way things worked out, we didn't have classes together in sixth grade, so it wasn't a problem.

"The other thing that made me feel things would be okay was that when school started there was a girl named Anna who sat next to me, and she seemed to be a really good, nice person, like someone I might be friends with. As it turned out, we both were signed up to attend ballroom dancing classes after school at a very traditional club. Since Anna lived far downtown and I lived near the club where the dance classes were being held, Anna started coming to my house after school on dance nights. She'd have dinner with my family, and then we could walk to dance class. Then Anna's parents would pick both of us up after class, drop me off at home, then drive downtown to their house. We did that every week we had dance class for all four years of the program, and it became totally natural that we would be together every other Thursday. Classes were more fun because I had Anna there, and since there were some girls in the class who were Anna's friends, they became my friends by association.

"Anna has been my best friend ever since. We're not in classes together this year, but we spend our lunch breaks, vacations, school breaks together, and we do a lot of FaceTime. I think our friendship is so strong because we have a lot of things in common. We're both kind of intellectual, we're both studious, and we're both focused on doing the right thing. I'd say we don't share real hobbies, but our interests complement each other, and we can always give each other helpful feedback. For instance, Anna is very into both sports and the stage; she had a decision to make about which she had to focus on— whether to continue with sports, or to do drama. I convinced her to go out for the school play, and she turned out to get the lead in the play!"

Hattie summed up, "I think our friendship is so strong because we push each other; we challenge each other in good ways. I think we bring out the best in each other, whatever that is."

One element that recurred often when I spoke with young people about best friends was the importance of mutual support. What does support, or being supportive, mean? Being there—being present for your friend—was mentioned often. Putting one's own needs aside in order to be there for a friend: going for a walk when they needed to talk, comforting them when things were looking dark, standing up for them when they needed an ally—these were the qualities, the actions, which young people described as being most important to them in a true friendship. And, they told me, that support should be reciprocal—they not only wanted their friend to be there for *them*, they wanted to be there for their friend.

Some young people have more than one person they consider a best friend. Sometimes the friendship is individual, where one person is close friends with several different people but those people are not close friends with each other, and sometimes the various best friends are equally close with each other. As Sara told me, "I have three best friends; they're amazing in every way. The first I met in kindergarten, and we've been best friends ever since. The second I met in second grade; when we were split up the next year, and ended up in different classes, we drifted apart. But then once we got to middle school, we became best friends again. The third, Karen, I met in third grade; she and I talk on the phone every night. My three best friends weren't all originally as close with each other as they were with me, but then two of them went to camp together and became close with each other, and I'd say that now we're all equally close."

Sara continued: "I think that it's unusual that there are four of us who are really, really close friends. I think of them all as my best friends. For me, the most important thing has been that the four of us connected. I've been close to my best friend Karen since third grade, and it's incredible and wonderful to have one amazing friend.

But for the past three years, it's been amazing having *three* really, really close friends. I know that I can talk to all three of them, and I also know that if I only get to talk to one, there are still those other two people I can really rely on as well."

Kate, a seventeen-year-old who lives in Upstate New York, described that wonderful feeling when two people "click." "I think finding a best friend is sometimes a chance thing. It may be based on what you have in common. It's an amazing feeling when you meet someone and you just kind of click. But I also know that it can take meeting a lot of people to find that click. It took a long time for me to find people I really clicked with. And the important thing in that sense is not to give up. Because you *will* find somebody you have a lot in common with."

Kate had a lot of insight into how and why she was able to find some close friendships. "I always feel the best part of meeting someone new is learning about them; I just really like learning about people. That's why making new friends is always really exciting to me. And then, for me, finding a common interest, and then taking what you can do and what the other person can do and putting it together is where a greater friendship comes along. That's where hanging out together comes in, taking something that you both have in common and then putting it together so you can both do it. In other words, taking something that you would do alone—and doing it together. For example, when I moved to Upstate New York, I met this one girl because my friend back home knew her, and so she was part of our online friend group, and then I met her in person when I moved here. And we became really close, but it took a long time because she was really quiet. It took almost a year to start to get to know her because she really didn't talk that much. But then, when we got closer, I found that this girl can talk for hours! It turns out she was shy, very shy. I just had this feeling from the beginning that I wanted to get to know her better; I couldn't exactly explain why. But because she was always quiet, I didn't know whether she would even want to become friends, so I didn't know how to approach her. I even told my mom, 'I want to become friends with Addie,' and she encouraged me to make an effort to do that. And it was one of the best things I've ever done, becoming friends with her. We really got to know each other, and she's been really the constant the whole time I've been here. She's the number one person I've been with the whole time. And so that's why I would say, if you want to be friends with somebody, 'Go for it!'"

Henry pointed out how sometimes background and similarities are an important factor in how close a friendship becomes—as is parental approval. "My parents want to know who my friends are, and I guess most parents do. There was this one guy who used to live near me, and he was very nice and had really good manners and we were really great friends—and I know that my parents really liked him, and, in a way, that made me appreciate him more. But among the other guys I know, some of their families do things differently than mine does, and I think my parents aren't very comfortable with that, and so I tend not to get that friendly with them." Sara echoed Henry's experience. "There are some kids in my class who I know my parents would not necessarily want me to be friends with, and I do get it; so for now, my parents approve of all my friends."

While adult approval, whether that of parents or teachers, can influence how friendships play out, in Ben's experience, it was important to weigh such input and make a decision for himself. "There are some guys who are really nice, really genuine, but we don't have similar backgrounds. I had a teacher who suggested once that perhaps I shouldn't hang out with a certain kid, but he was my friend and had been for a while. I didn't think the teacher really knew him well, and in my opinion, my friend was a good guy. I think that you know when a friendship is real; to me, a real friendship is generally one that can last more than a year. I'm still really good friends with that guy, and the teacher's come around to agreeing with me that he's a good guy."

There are many ways that people recognize true friendships, and many ways to keep friendships ongoing and vibrant. But as I talked to young people about friendship, I heard versions of the same sentiments echoed over and over again by everyone with whom I spoke.

As one young woman summed it up, "Real friends bring out the best in you, and they always have your back."

6

WHEN FRIENDSHIP FAILS

Friendships can be great, especially in their endless variety. They can be casual, they can be deep, they can be short term, and they can last a lifetime. But there are times when friendships are tested, or end unhappily—sometimes by choice, and sometimes as the result of a disagreement, a misunderstanding, a fight, or a hurtful comment. And sometimes a relationship looks like friendship but is actually harmful—what is often called a "toxic friendship." There are many reasons why friendships fail, and reasons why people find themselves in relationships that are hurtful or toxic. It is almost always uncomfortable, both for those involved and for those who see it happen. As Grace put it, "I've seen some of these so-called friendships; sometimes it's not quite obvious at first that it's not working, but once you hear about it, then you realize that there've been all these little signs that it wasn't good, and it's like, 'Oh, I see what you mean, there's something really bizarre about their friendship.' And it's really sad to see other people fight, or be mean to each other, especially when they're supposed to be friends, because, well, everyone knows how that feels, and no one likes that feeling."

While people of any age are usually saddened by the breakup of a friendship, social scientists have come to see that the adolescent brain reacts more strongly to certain social stimuli than does the adult brain. As Lydia Denworth writes in her book *Friendship*, "It actually hurts more to be rejected in adolescence than at any other age."[1] Indeed, broken friendships can leave lasting hurt, and toxic friendships can be dangerous. By thinking about your own friendships, or those of your peers, you might begin to see patterns or evidence of friendships that are not healthy, or helpful in any way.

TOXIC, HURTFUL, OR FAKE FRIENDSHIPS

There are times when a person seems to be a friend, but at some point in your relationship with them you find that—unlike a true friend—they just don't make you feel happy or relaxed. It may be because they tease you or put you down. It may be that they're always making things "about them" rather than being interested in you and what you might have to say. Whether they are simply not very nice people or they turn out to have motives other than genuine friendship behind their interactions with you, such a relationship can be confusing and emotionally stressful. As seventeen-year-old Kate put it wisely, "Toxic friendships are just not of value, are of no use, and are usually downright hurtful." Sometimes, she said, people seem to stumble into them, or even willingly get drawn into a really negative friendship. And that's not hard, she pointed out, because "it's easy to get drawn in, especially when there are things you really like about that person." So how do you recognize a "fake" or "toxic" friendship?

Kate's Story

Unfortunately, I've had some experience with what I think of as bad friendships. In my view, there are some signs pointing to whether a friendship is good, or whether it's really not a friendship but some twisted kind of relationship. For instance, when it seems that another person only seems to be your friend when they need something from you, that should tip you off and make you question whether this so-called friend is really a friend. Also, when you have a relationship where you actually have to ask yourself that question, then what you have is not a real friendship. But is it a toxic friendship? Ask yourself, does this person bring you down or make you feel sad when you're around them? Or does it make you nervous to be with them, like you have to walk on eggshells when you are with them, in case they will blow up at something? Another clue to whether a friendship is dangerous is when someone you thought of as a friend tries to get you to do something you don't want to do.

I know that when I've been in that type of relationship, I've sometimes felt that doing one thing wrong—or saying something wrong—would have set the other person off. And I was always so worried about that because, basically, I liked that person for a reason. And that's the hardest part about toxic friendships, because most of the time you got into that relationship in the first place because you liked something about the other person, but then you find that you don't like certain parts of them or certain things they do. The other thing that I've noticed about toxic friendships is that there are times when they're really good, and times when they're really bad. I think that generally has to do with personal issues that the other person has, I guess, which play into their lives and makes them so difficult to be with. I find that's kind of sad, but you have to realize that it happens, and that it may not be a healthy relationship for you to be in. And my best advice, for someone who feels like they are in that kind of a situation, as difficult as it may be, is to just leave. It's a very difficult thing, in a sad, sad sense, to just walk away from a friendship. But when the friendship—if you want to call it that—is hurtful, or makes you nervous, it's just not good for you and not a real friendship. So, ultimately, you may just have to walk away.

* * *

Most of us want friendships. And when we are eager to make friends, it can be very easy to be taken in by someone who pretends to hold out the hand of friendship but is only doing it as part of a game, or with even worse intentions. Jordana described a situation she experienced that illustrated how some young people make a game of preying on others in the guise of making friends. "When I went to camp a few years ago," Jordana explained, "I didn't know any of the kids in advance. When I got there, I met these two girls who were friends with each other, and I thought it would be a good idea to make friends with them. I was *so* clueless! They seemed nice, and I thought they were pretty cool. But then, a day later, when we were on the bus going home, they started bugging me, teasing me, I guess, telling me that I would need to bring them a gift the next day if I wanted to be their friend. And they started getting really rude and just badgering me about it, and telling me that they were going to make sure the other girls wouldn't be friends with me if I didn't bring them what they wanted. And then the next day, I had my backpack with me because it had my lunch in it, and as soon as I got to camp they came up to me and started saying they were going to search my backpack to see if I'd brought their present. And they were really aggressive, and I just said, 'Hey, you said you wanted to be friends with me, but that's not how friends act, so knock it off!' And they didn't search my backpack, and they just lost interest in me, I guess, and never bothered me again. But I certainly didn't become friends with them. My perspective just flipped around; at first they seemed so sweet, and nice, and then it's like—Bam!—it hit me in the face: these were definitely not kids I wanted to be friends with. I think what I learned from that is that there are fake friendships, or bad friendships, and I just want to stay away from that. There are people out there that you might not click with, who are rude or just not nice, and if there's someone pushing you around, like in an on-again-off-again friendship, that's not a real friendship, and you've got to just say no or get out of that situation."

Kate explained her theory about what she calls fake friendships, how and why they develop, and how she feels about them. "Humans tend to be negative, and when people are negative, I don't want to be around them. Kids who are very negative, who shut themselves away emotionally, giving off the vibe that 'I hate everybody,' that's a very common thing for a teenager to say; well, I tend to stay away from people like that, because I don't want any part of that. And then there are kids who are also just plain mean; it seems like there is no gratification for them, no reason for being mean, and I see that a lot: in people my age, being mean for no reason is very common. And I would recommend staying away from those people in the first place, because when it comes to friendship with people who are mean, what I've noticed among kids my age is that they're not just going to be mean to other people—they can turn on you, too. And then it tends to get very bad, very quickly; then you are trapped.

"The other thing I've noticed," Kate continued, "is that when people think you're beneath them, don't even start hanging out with them. When they act like they're superior to you, that's another time when making an effort to be friends isn't worth it. There are some people who think they're so above you that they don't have to put any effort into friendship. And it happens a lot, I guess, among the more popular people in our school. They tend to float above the others, like they're in their own egotistical heads. I think ego is a big mistake when it comes to friendship. If you are egotistical about yourself in the sense that you think you're better than other people, that's when someone loses me as a friend.

"I've also seen a lot of instances of what I think of as fake friends. Like when someone is friends with someone they don't really like, but they don't want to hurt their feelings by ending the friendship because they've known each other for a while. So they kind of keep leading then on, acting like they like them, even when they don't. And I think that's really hurting the other person."

When Teasing Turns Hurtful

We have all been teased, probably more than once during our lives. Older siblings tease younger ones, parents may tease a child out of a bad mood, and friends can tease each other with affection and humor or even as a form of flirting. Most of us know how to respond to gentle or affectionate teasing with good humor—whether with a quick quip, by teasing back or laughing, or by throwing a pillow or launching into roughhousing. But sometimes teasing is hurtful; teasing that is intentionally hurtful is a form of bullying.

When someone whom you thought of as a friend finds a way to tease you that hurts, it can be particularly painful. Was it an unintentional wound? A close friend generally knows your sensitive spots and may think they're being affectionately funny when they touch on a sore spot. A real friend will be contrite and apologize if they realize they've hurt you, and hopefully you will understand, accept it, and be able to move on. But a bully may also know what you are especially sensitive about—whether it's your height, your weight, or some other personal detail—and intentionally probe at that sensitivity with a barbed tease. That is *not* friendship, though it may be disguised as such. Being able to distinguish what the intent of the teasing is can help you recognize a "friend" is a bully.

BROKEN FRIENDSHIPS

Sometimes a friendship sours because of a misunderstanding; it may be possible to heal such a situation, but a friendship that has suffered a break cannot always be mended. As one young woman told me, "A broken friendship hurts. Sometimes it's not a huge deal, but it still stings a little bit."

Judith described a situation she found herself in. "I had a group of friends, and we would get together a lot to play *Minecraft*. There was one girl in the group and I thought we were pretty good friends, but then one day, out of the blue, she just blew up, yelling that I'd smirked wrong at one of the other kids. I didn't smirk at all! But she convinced my friends that I had, and they all ganged up against me, and I just got up and left. That was a horrible day, and I just didn't know what had gotten into her. The next day she apologized, and I've gotten back to playing *Minecraft* with them, but I just don't feel the same way about her. It's like I feel she could just pull something like that another time, and I don't want to be on the receiving end again."

Occasionally, it's not what happens to you that makes a friendship dissolve but what you realize about someone from how they treat other people. Henry put it thoughtfully: "What makes a person become not a friend? An unfriend? Sometimes it's seeing how they treat someone else. I had a situation where this guy who I thought was my friend was being not that nice to my best friend Jake; he was being really forceful about something with Jake, and I just had this sudden realization that he wasn't a nice guy after all. If he could be like that with Jake, it meant he could be like that with anybody, just plain mean. We sort of fell out after that; we didn't have a fight or anything, but we're not friends anymore. It kind of happened naturally; you start to have different interests, not to hang out as much, and start to drift apart. But I just lost any feeling of being friends with him after I saw how he treated Jake."

For some people, it is an unintentional slight that causes a break in friendship. Morgan described such an incident among her group of friends. "I have a close group of girlfriends, and we're all pretty much equally friends with each other. A while back, though, we had a school assignment to write about what was hardest for us during the pandemic, and I did a video all about how what I missed most was not being able to see my closest friends Ellis and Phoebe. Except unfortunately I didn't mention another girl, Liza, in the video, and that upset her, and she wrote me a really harsh email. I felt very bad about it, but in truth, when I made the video, I really was thinking only about Ellis and Phoebe. I called Liza and tried to explain, and we were able to sort of straighten it out, but we're not really such good friends anymore. That was not one of my best experiences with friendship."

For many young people, trust is a tremendous part of close friendship. And just as not all broken friendships are mended, not all betrayals can be forgiven. While Morgan's unfortunate experience was not intentional, there are situations where a friendship sours because of an intentional breach of trust, or an outright betrayal. Ben hasn't had such issues with really close friends, but he has seen it happen with others and has even tried to mediate. "There were a couple of guys in school who had gotten into a huge issue because one of them accused the other of telling everyone something about him that was not true. I was friends with each of them, and so I went to each one separately to try to talk it out, sort out what was wrong between them, and encourage them to give it a little time and work it out. But they were just not going to get over it. And I saw how the concept of being betrayed, of someone going behind your back, can definitely ruin a relationship. It's a sour thing to do, and can definitely hurt a relationship. Some people can forgive that; others can take it to the grave."

In Tali's case, feeling betrayed by a good friend has left her feeling vulnerable. "I had a good friend when I lived in California. We were really close, and I told her something in confidence—I told her that I had a crush on this guy in our class. And she went and actually told my crush that I liked him. Maybe it seems kind of silly, but I really felt betrayed by her; it wasn't just that I was embarrassed that he knew how I felt, but that I'd told her something important to me, trusting that it wouldn't go any further, and then she just turned on me. I was furious and didn't want to have anything more to do with her. I didn't feel like I could trust her. I still see her in school, and we say hello and stuff, but we don't hang out, and I don't feel like I can ever really be friends with her again."

In Jimmy's experience, a breach of trust challenged a friendship but wasn't necessarily irreparable. As Jimmy described, " I once had the experience that someone I'm friendly with—not one of my closest friends—spread rumors about me that weren't true. I knew they weren't true, and he knew they weren't true. I don't know why he did that; maybe he thought it was a joke, maybe just for no reason. But I did feel betrayed, because we'd hung out a little, and I thought we were friends. It certainly wasn't a good feeling, and it's a tough situation to be in. I didn't understand why he did it, and I was really upset. But I felt like we were still friends, because I do like him, and I wanted to keep being friends with him. So I talked it through with him, and he ended up apologizing, and I decided to leave it at that. I basically decided it just didn't matter, because in school, something like that goes around for a week, and you might feel down about it, but the next week something else will happen and then that's all anyone is talking about, and they'll forget about your thing. So I decided not to let it bother me, because I thought this guy was basically a good guy, and I wanted to stay friends with him. But if someone else had done something like that, and kept doing it, then that would ruin the relationship. I think that would be a fake friendship, or a toxic friendship—not really a friendship at all."

As Jimmy's story illustrates, having trust in a friend is an important factor in feeling that a friendship is genuine. Judith explained her feelings this way: "I think maybe the most important thing in a friendship is being able to trust the other person. By that, I mean being able to tell them things, personal things, and know that they won't tell everyone, or put it on BuzzFeed Gossip. That didn't happen to me, but it did happen to one of my friends, and she was devastated. I don't know who did it, but I have my suspects."

Hattie's experience with a close friendship that was tested had a happier ending than some others. As she explained, "My close friendship with Anna was tested last year—it was really the only fight we've had. We had a history teacher whom everyone seemed to have a crush on, but for some reason, he didn't like me, which made it a very strange and stressful time for me and created a strange class dynamic. Anna understood how stressful it was for me; she didn't have a crush on the teacher like all the other girls did. And then, for one history project, we were all paired off into teams of two to work on presentations, and Anna and I chose to do ours about ancient coins. That turned out to be a bad idea because the school library didn't have many resources to use, and we couldn't find a whole lot of information online. So we were getting really stressed out about our presentation, especially because I felt the teacher had it in for me, and then the day of the presentation came, and we didn't feel prepared, and we were really snapping at each other and before class we had a big fight about what we were going to do. We thought the presentation was terrible, but we actually got an A. Maybe because the stress was off, maybe because we actually did well, but we were able to make up, and in the long run, our friendship didn't suffer. If anything, we're better friends than ever."

Sara described what it was like for her: "No one's really betrayed me," she said, "but there was definitely a group of kids who I thought were my friends, and then—I wouldn't say they betrayed me—but all of a sudden, one day it was like they didn't exactly welcome me either. We would be together, talking, and when I would say something they would sort of ignore it, or tell me I was wrong. It would have been one thing if they had a different opinion than me about something—that's fine—but this was more like just shutting me out. And I think that a real friend would still try to include someone, and not let the group shut them down; so I wouldn't say they betrayed me, but I would say it was not that great, and it did not feel like friendship."

Grace talked about how broken friendships can hurt but can sometimes result in positive changes. "I had a friend who I'd known since elementary school. We were such great friends, but then we started not getting along, and I don't really know why. I won't say we had fights, but we definitely started arguing about things, and as things went on, we never really got along that well anymore. It's really unfortunate, because we were so close for so long, and it feels really terrible, at first, to realize you're not friends anymore. But I think it just means that you'll go on and meet other people, who appreciate you, and when that happens, it just means that maybe that first one wasn't the right person for you to be friends with anymore."

CLIQUES: WHO'S IN AND WHO'S OUT

One of the most common situations in adolescent and teenage years is the formation of cliques—groups who stick together with some exclusivity, resulting in some kids being "in" and some being "out." That can yield very uncomfortable, even hurt, feelings, especially when who's in and who's out turns out to be somewhat fluid.

In her book *Friendship*, author Lydia Denworth writes, "What so defines friendship in adolescence . . . are the larger alliances. Beyond pairs of friends, there are groups of perhaps three to ten. You could call them cliques. They can be hierarchical, or they can be roughly egalitarian." She goes on to mention the categories so prevalent in teen movies, such as the jocks, the nerds, and the theater kids, and points out that while that is a "Disney version of reality, it wasn't all that far from what most teenagers experience."[2] As Sara said, "In my school, it was very obvious who was the 'popular group,' and people want to be friends with them even if they weren't so nice; they just start wanting to be in with a certain group of kids, even if they don't have that much in common." For many kids, cliques present the very real possibility of uncomfortable interactions.

Emily described the appeal of being in the right clique. "There's a pretty big group of girls in my school who have always been considered the popular kids. A lot of people want to be friends with them, even if that group is not really so nice. It's just that the other kids think it would be cool to be friends with them and to be in their clique. That group always starts the trends at school, and some of those trends just seem pretty stupid to me. But to some kids—the kids who want in—it's like something they dream about."

Cliques, particularly in adolescent years, can be a testing ground for friendships—and sometimes a particularly destructive one. As Cipi put it rather dramatically, "In middle school, the girls could be really cold and backstabbing. You might be in a friendship, but the second the more popular girls decide they don't like you, then suddenly the person you think is your friend might decide they have a choice: 'Okay, this is survival in middle school; do I bond with my old friend and stand up to these more popular girls, or do I side with them, become one of them, and let my friend get hurt while I survive?' I think that's the test of real friendship: your real friend will stick by you, defend you, deciding 'I don't want to become one of them.' These situations happen a lot—sad but true. Middle school can be like a war zone."

While possibly more common with adolescent girls, cliques and other exclusive groups are hard for young men as well. Trying to maintain exclusivity, or trying to figure out who's in and who's out, can cause problems with anyone's friendships. This was the case in

Jimmy's experience. As he told me, "There was a boy in our school who we really didn't like that much. He was new, and he tried to join our group. He didn't really fit in, but we couldn't just come out and tell him we didn't want him there, so he ended up sticking around, but not really joining us. And I noticed that my group of friends kind of treated him differently than they treated each other. Like, when one of them was passing around their phone to show something on it, they'd skip him. I really didn't know how to get around the problem; I didn't want to just tell him that he didn't fit into our group, but I felt if we didn't, we were just leading him on. I think it's a tough situation either way.

"Ultimately, he kind of got the picture and drifted away. I think that's the best way this kind of situation could resolve. I don't know what we would have done if he didn't figure it himself, because he wouldn't ever really be one of our circle, even if he just hung around. So I guess it ended in the best way, without any ugliness."

Jimmy continued, "It's hard to know what to do, because what happens is that if you're trying to fit into one group, then kids in the other groups start thinking of you as part of that group. And if it doesn't work out, it's hard to move into a different group, because the other kids have kind of designated you already as part of the first group you tried to join. Maybe that kind of thing doesn't happen at other schools, but it seems to be the way it is at ours. And that's why I think, especially for new kids, joining extracurriculars is a good way to find the right group, a group that has your same interests, before you try to fit yourself into a group of kids."

Kate shared similar thoughts about groups and the difficulties that arise when someone doesn't seem to fit in. "I've seen instances where there's a group of friends, and someone else kind of forces their way into the group. Even if none of the other kids like that person, it's hard for them to tell the person they don't really fit in. You would think that someone would figure it out for themselves, but when they don't, you don't just tell that person you can't hang out with us, so it ends up that the kid no one likes kind of stays there, and then it usually gets tougher and tougher for them to fit in. For example, they probably don't get invited to the exclusive parties and stuff, even though the rest of the group does. So I kind of think of that as a group of fake friends, and I've seen that more than once."

Sara described very clearly how cliques can be hurtful—even when one is not interested in joining the group. "There have always been cliques in my school, and there was always the so-called popular group. Kids were always trying to get into the popular group, which happened to be a bunch of kids who played basketball together, so some of the kids would go out for the basketball team just to join the group. I wasn't trying to get into the group, but I was on the basketball team. And I think it was hard, because they were all friends, and you're on a team with them, but it doesn't really feel like a team because they're excluding you. But I felt I wasn't like them; I didn't wear the same kind of clothes they did, and I didn't really fit in, and they let me know it. There were times when I felt deliberately excluded. For instance, there was a pizza store near school, and when we had an away game, they'd go to get pizza to eat before the bus left. And no one would text me about the pizza, and then it was weird when they'd all come in with their boxes of pizza. It wasn't that I wanted pizza, but I didn't like feeling left out. They weren't outright mean to me, but they made a point of leaving me out. And that was harsh."

While Sara didn't know whether the girls' exclusion of her was deliberate or unintentional, one of the uglier sides of cliques is that sometimes those in the group seem oblivious to the feelings of those outside or, even worse, deliberately seem to want to hurt them with teasing or aggressive behavior. Sara's sister described just such an experience: "Last year, a lot of the kids were doing TikToks. My parents didn't let me do TikToks, and I had no interest in doing TikToks, but every day on the school bus, the kids in that group would make TikToks. Okay, that was fine—it was a little annoying because they were really loud about it—but, fine, they could do whatever they want with their TikToks. But one day they started to do a group TikTok, trying to get everyone in on it, and I said, 'No, I really don't want to. I'm not comfortable with that. I don't want to be on it.' And they just started shoving a phone in my face, pushing me to do it, too. It was just so stupid. I wouldn't say it's humiliating, but it made me feel really uncomfortable because I didn't want to do it with them, and they were being so pushy and just not listening to me or caring what I thought."

Having the strength of character to say no to something you don't want to do, especially when you are facing peer pressure to do it, can be one of the hardest challenges of the teen years. Being able to stand up for yourself, stick to your principles, and stay true to your own feelings and beliefs is a step toward a healthy adulthood.

RIVALRIES AND JEALOUSY

Sometimes what causes a friendship to fail is a sense of rivalry or jealousy that develops, despite good intentions. Cipi explained what happened when she tried to bring together an old friend and a newer friend. "Last year I had a situation where two of my friendships turned into a tug-of-war. I had been friends with this girl, Esme, since kindergarten. We weren't best friends, but since we'd known each other so long, we were pretty close. And then when I met Jordi, we became best friends almost instantly, and we were together all the time. And I had what I thought was a great idea, which was to bring my two friends together. Jordi and I often went to the baseball stadium together, and we always had a great time, so I decided to invite Esme to come join us once. So we were all at the stadium, and Jordi was being really nice, but Esme was just being kind of weird and cold, and she was on her phone the whole time. I feel that screens, and being on your phone, kind of take away from spending time with your friends, so I had this conflict. And I asked Esme, 'Do you like the game?,' and her response was, 'Whatever,' and she just went back to her phone. I was kind of bummed, because I thought, 'Hey, I invited you!' But Jordi cheered me up, as usual, and we had a great time. But later, Jordi told me that she actually hadn't liked that scene at all; she said she'd felt like Esme was coming between us, since I'd known Esme since kindergarten and I had just met Jordi recently. And even though Jordi felt like we had this really strong connection, she also felt like Esme was taking me away from her. That made me feel really bad, because I would never do that to Jordi, and I felt much closer to her than to Esme. But that got me to thinking that probably the reason Esme was so weird that day was because she would have been happier if it was only me and her. So she was just giving me and Jordi the cold shoulder. I guess she was feeling kind of left out, or even jealous, because me and Jordi were such good friends. And I felt like I was in a tug-of-war between my two friends. The end of the story is that I don't really see Esme anymore; I transferred away from the school we both went to, and we haven't attempted to get together since then."

Another young woman described a situation where transfer to a new school kindled feelings of jealousy with an old friend. "I had a really good friend, and we were going to transfer to a new school together at the same time. As it turned out, I transferred a month before she did, so I started making some new friends before she got there. Then, when she did enroll, I think she felt a little competitive with me, because we were both new students, but I already had some friends in that school. And she started giving me the cold shoulder; she wouldn't text me and she started humiliating me in class, like when I said something she would sigh and roll her eyes and act like I'd said something dumb. And I really think it was because she felt like I'd made new friends and left her behind. Which wasn't true, because I would have been perfectly happy bringing her in with my new group, but she just made it so hard, and I finally just stopped trying. I felt bad about it, and I tried to talk with her about it, but she just acted snappy and told me to go off with my new friends. So I did."

Healthy friendships are one of the most wonderful experiences of life, while unhealthy ones can cause lasting damage and pain. Learning how to recognize real friendship, deal with difficult situations among people, and acknowledge, and end, a hurtful or toxic relationship are important steps toward adulthood. Grace had some important thoughts about how to navigate difficult interpersonal situations, based on her experience. "There was a time when some of the kids in my class were being really difficult to me; it was kind of teasing but with a nasty edge. I was feeling very shut out and didn't understand what was going on. So I went to some other kids in the class who I knew were really above that kind of stuff, who weren't included in it, and I just kind of explained to them what was happening. I felt that they would understand where I'm coming from, and they did; their response was 'Don't worry about them; you don't want to get mixed up in that kind of drama. Just ignore them, and they'll stop.' So I did, and they never really bothered me again. Sometimes it just helps to talk to someone who's outside of that group."

Part Three

What's Next?

7

WHAT YOU LEARN FROM FRIENDSHIP

Friendship is not just a relationship, or an activity. Friendship also teaches us about life, makes us realize things we might not have known about ourselves—or others—and friendship can also sometimes surprise us or challenge our assumptions. Here are some of the truths the young people I spoke with realized about friendship.

SOMETIMES OPPOSITES MAKE THE BEST FRIENDS

Some people have friends who are very like them—what attracts them to each other in the first place may be that they recognize similarities in themselves. For other people, having a friend whose personality complements theirs by being different may add spark and contrast that enliven the relationship. Cipi explained how that worked for her.

"I would say," Cipi considered, "that in a friendship, people play different roles. In my friendship with Jordi, I'm more the chatterbox and Jordi's more the calm, thoughtful one. In my experience, it works best if, for example, your personality is talkative and bubbly, you might feel best with someone who is the opposite. It seems to me that if both of you are bubbly personalities, it's like you're too much the same. If you're the quiet one, you should look for someone who's more talkative, who can do more of the talking in a conversation. In my opinion, that just balances things better."

HOW YOUR PARENTS VIEW YOUR FRIENDS CAN MAKE A DIFFERENCE

A big part of growing up is making friends who introduce you to new ideas and ways of doing things, steps toward the growing independence of adulthood. But even as you grow more independent during adolescence and the teen years, your parents are probably still paying some attention to your social environment (perhaps more than you'd wish!), and the way they feel about your friends can color the way you feel about those relationships.

"My parents love my friends!" laughed Jordana. "And I love introducing my friends to my parents. Before the pandemic, when I used to be able to have friends come over to our house and have sleepovers, and I'd introduce a friend to my mom, it was kind of my friend's time to shine—and my mom's time to shine! It gave me a chance to see how they'd react to each other, and to me. And it was great to watch my mom in action with my friends. She's really good at sizing someone up, and I knew that if *she* liked them, that's a go."

And as Sylvia found, "A lot of my friends have parents who are friends of my parents. It makes it easy to be with them, because my parents know them and—at least before Covid—they made it easy to get together. My parents like some of my other friends, and some they just don't have any opinion about. But they're usually pretty on target about the kids I'm friends with."

Tali's case is similar: many of her parents' friends are parents of her own friends. And, she added, "My parents like all of my friends. Since most of my good friends' parents are really good friends of my parents, they like the parents, and then they like the kids. So that works!"

Sara found that when her parents knew and liked her friends' parents, things usually went smoothly. But, she said, "Some of the kids that I am friends with—I wouldn't say close friends, but maybe a little bit more than acquaintances—my parents do not particularly like. I wouldn't say that they don't want me to be friends with them, but they definitely don't like them, and I kind of know what they mean. Maybe that's why I think of them as acquaintances more than friends."

And for Grace, "I have friends my parents have loved, and I've had friends my parents have been a little wary of. And surprisingly, it always turns out that the ones my mom likes the best are always the ones that I keep—and it never has to do with my mom's decision; it's just how it always turns out. Sometimes my mom has let me know, kind of carefully, something like, 'I like this person, but I don't really know about their attitude, or their judgment,' or something like that, and I'll be like, 'Are you kidding? Don't say that about my friend!,' and over the course of time I realize, 'Oh, yeah, she was right about them!'"

Kate has a very close relationship with her mother, and that relationship has helped her with all kinds of friendships. As Kate explained, "I'm actually quite open with my mother, probably more than most teenagers. Some kids actually find it unnerving that I'm so close to my mom, but I find it one of the most wonderful things that you can have as a teenager. My mom has given me some good advice, and I've actually stayed safer than I would have been without her advice. And even though she's an adult, she was a teenager once, and knows what that's like, even as different as it is now than when she was younger. She knows the friendship aspect, and really gets what I am going through. I think that's one thing that kids forget, and take for granted, that their parents were once teenagers, too, and probably have a pretty good idea about what you're going through.

"There have been times when my mom suggested that someone was not the right friend for me. But I can be an unruly teenager, and sometimes I don't listen, and of course insisted they were great. But naturally, turns out she was right—she's always right! And one thing I've found is that my mom tends to realize way before I do when something's not right; that may be because she is just very socially intelligent in the first place. For example, I had a boyfriend who was quite awful, actually, and my mom was probably the first person to tell me, 'Hey, something's off, something's not working there,' and that I should be careful with him. Did I listen? Not at first, but eventually, yes, because she really was right!"

SHARING IS A BIG PART OF FRIENDSHIP

Whether you are sharing a snack, a secret, or a special language, the act of sharing something is an important part of the closeness of friendship. For Cipi, nicknames were important. "Nicknames are very important in a friendship," Cipi told me. "It makes it kind of a secret, something you share with your friend. My best friend and I have nicknames for each other, which we basically made up, and it's really cool, and a big part of our friendship. We also make up words—it's like having a secret language—and that keeps us laughing and bonds us together."

DON'T JUDGE PEOPLE BY WHAT OTHERS THINK

It is hard, sometimes, not to be swayed by what others think. But part of growing up is learning to make independent decisions, to decide things for yourself, and not to let others influence the way you may think of someone.

In Henry's experience, "One thing that I've learned is that very often kids judge each other by social status, and just superficial things. For them, it's not about who you really are; it's about how you look, things about you that are on the outside, not on the inside. And I've seen that some kids don't want to be friends with someone who they think seems weird on the outside, or different from them. But some of those folks, who the others think are weird, have turned out to be some of my best friends; when I get to know them, I find out that they're really cool, in their own special way."

HENRY'S STORY

There was this one new girl in my class this year, and I could tell that she was trying to be cool, to be just like every other girl in the grade, but she was really different, and seemed kind of weird. After a while, I could see that the other kids weren't interested in getting to know her, and everyone was kind of avoiding her, because they thought she was weird. But for a class writing project, we had to write to someone in class, and she was the one I was assigned to write to. And—this was all on Zoom, during Covid—when we had a Zoom breakout session together, I got to talking with her, and found that when she was just being her own self, not trying to be like the others, she was really nice, and really interesting. And now we're friends. And it showed me that it was crazy to try and be a person you're not, just to get in with other people. She was trying to be someone she wasn't, and nobody was impressed. But when I got to know her, when she was just herself, she was great.

KEEPING IN TOUCH WITH FRIENDS IS IMPORTANT

It can be very easy to take friendship for granted. We see our friends, we spend time with them, and we may just assume that's the way it will always be. But friendships needs to be kept alive in order to thrive, and sometimes that takes intention, determination, and some effort.

"Keeping in touch with your friends is so important," Judith says. "When I used to talk with my best friend, especially during the summer when we didn't have school, we'd talk multiple times a day. On days when we did have school, it was more like a few times a week, because we weren't going to the same school. But now, with the pandemic, I feel it's so much more important to keep in contact with each other, so we talk all the time on the phone. It's what keeps us feeling close. Usually it's only for ten or fifteen minutes, but my ultimate all-time record is two hours."

After Henry was assigned a project with the new girl at school, he realized
that when she was just being herself, she was really interesting and nice.

IT'S IMPORTANT TO HAVE THINGS IN COMMON

As pointed out elsewhere, much of friendship is based on having things in common. Whether it is a hobby, a sport, a TV show that you both love, or some other affiliation, common interests draw us together, give us something to talk about, and bond friendships.

Morgan, a young teen, pointed out how common interests keep her and her best friends close. "It's important for friends to have things in common. For instance, my two best friends, Phoebe and Ellis, and I all have siblings, so we know what it's like, and we laugh and complain a lot about it. And we like a lot of the same things—we like the same kind of clothes, like jean shorts and cool shirts. We love animals, and we just enjoy the same kinds of things. And it's those things that we have in common that make us so close."

FRIENDSHIPS CAN COME AND GO

Some friendships last a lifetime, but other friendships fade or disappear altogether. Being able to appreciate a friendship in the moment can add depth and significance to that relationship, especially if you recognize that even a close friendship might come to an end. And being able to deal with the ebb and flow of friendships can give us a more secure footing with relationships in general.

"One thing I've learned," Hattie reminisced, "is that you have to expect that friendships come and go, that you can't rely on them to last forever, although you could be lucky. But I think it's not uncommon for friendships to dissolve over time, whether because you change schools, or move away, or just grow apart. It doesn't have to take an argument, or any kind of a fight; a friendship can just kind of undo."

FRIENDSHIPS ARE WONDERFUL, BUT ACQUAINTANCES ARE VALUABLE, TOO

When we are lucky enough to have good friends in our lives, our enjoyment of things is enhanced when we are with them. But we should not overlook the benefits of relationships with acquaintances or casual friends; they help fill our lives with diversity, interest, and socialization even when they are not emotionally close. Hattie explained how friends and acquaintances fill different roles in her life. "I've learned that friendship comes with time; it doesn't necessarily happen instantly. You should take advantage of circumstances; you don't have to try hard, but you should be open to letting it happen, and when it does, that's great. I also think that sometimes it's more important to have acquaintances than to have many friends. For me, for example, when I take tennis lessons, I can spend the hour without a close friend. But it is nice to have some tennis friends who are really just acquaintances; I don't think of them, in a way, as close friends, but I do enjoy being with them for just that hour during tennis lessons. We can laugh together, or share things about tennis, and that's an added benefit to the tennis lessons."

DEVELOPING A FRIENDSHIP TAKES ACTION

Even when a friendship seems to spark instantly or move along smoothly, it can still take effort to make it develop or keep it alive. As Emily said, "Sometimes you have to find ways to keep a friendship going. I find that if it's somebody that you go to school with, if you want to stay friends with them, one thing you can do is request that they be in your class, because being in the same class definitely helps. Also, you should definitely let someone know that you want to be their friend—it's not like just deciding, 'Oooh, I want to be friends with that person,' when she doesn't even know who you are. So you have to make it clear that you'd like to become friends, and keep being friends. Sit with them at lunch, arrange to meet outside of school, even ask them to join your club or team. It's not always easy, but it's worth the effort."

REAL FRIENDSHIP IS A TWO-WAY STREET

One thing that comes up often when talking about friendship is that friendship is a two-way street. It's not enough for one person to like another; the feeling has to be mutual. Similarly, there has to be give and take in the friendship, a reciprocity. Secrets can be shared, assistance can be offered—and taken—and honesty should be evident on both sides.

For Grace, "It's important to me that I know the friendship will go both ways. I've learned, from both experiencing it and hearing about it from others, how a one-sided friendship can be the worst and most pointless kind of friendship. I think friendship has to go both ways; the feelings of friendship have to be mutual. You have to both really like each other, get along well, and trust each other."

In Kate's experience, finding that a friendship was more one-sided than she thought changed one particular relationship. "I thought this one girl was a good friend, but then I realized that I was making more of an effort to keep our friendship going than she was. And that did hurt, but I think I'm better off knowing it. We still talk, but our relationship is not the same as it was. Because friendship is a very two-sided thing. You can't have one person trying to make it a thing, and then one person not. And in that sense, if it comes to the point that you're the only one trying to stay friends, then I think you're better off with better friends—because they *are* out there. That's also something that's hard to remember, especially if you feel you've lost a friend. But you have to keep in mind that there are other people out there who will like you, the same way that there will be people out there who won't like you—and that's okay. Not everybody has to like you, and not everybody has to be your friend."

MAKING FRIENDS DOESN'T HAVE TO BE HARD

As pointed out earlier, sometimes friendships "just happen." You sit down next to someone at a team tryout, and you end up being not just teammates but good friends. Or your mom took you to a playground when you were a toddler and ended up befriending another mother—and you two kids became close friends. For people who are naturally outgoing and vivacious, finding friends seems to happen instantly and often. But even for people who are less social, or more shy, making friends doesn't have to be hard.

"For me," Grace said, "I've learned that sometimes a friendship can start from just that first word; you can meet someone, start to talk, and from there, it all falls into place. But you have to have the courage to go up to someone and introduce yourself. I'd say that's something I've been pretty comfortable with, but it definitely takes confidence. I've found, though, that if you just show someone that you are interested in them, that you care, then that can really grab the other person's interest, and then they'll be drawn to you as well. So that's a great way to really get friendship started. And even if you're not really comfortable going up to people, don't be afraid to let people come up to you. And if they open a conversation, you just have to talk back."

YOU DON'T HAVE TO BE FRIENDS WITH EVERYONE

Some people feel that they should be friends with everyone—but there's no way that can work. People are different, people have different feelings about things, and not all personalities mesh well. But not being friends with everyone doesn't have to mean you can't be friendly, just as it doesn't mean that you shouldn't set limits or boundaries.

"Friendship has gotten me a lot of great things," said Kate. "And I think I'm naturally a friendly person. But I also know that one thing I have trouble with is remembering that I don't have to be best friends with everybody, and really, that you can't be. That's hard for me sometimes, because I just want to get to know everybody; that's just who I am. That's probably one of the harder parts about friendship. Realizing that you can't be best friends with everybody."

Just as Kate had to realize that she can't be friends with everyone, Grace had to find a way to deal kindly with someone whom she was not interested in befriending. "If there's someone wanting to be your friend, but you're not into it? I think the best thing to do is to be polite but a little closed off. You don't want to be rude and make them feel unwanted; you just have to find a polite way to not get involved further."

FRIENDSHIPS FLOURISH WHEN YOU DO THINGS TOGETHER

While having common interests is certainly an important factor in developing friendships, talking with friends is how we get to know people better. Sometimes, though, talking doesn't come easily; that's why actually engaging in activities together can be a valuable tool in deepening a friendship. As Jimmy discovered, shared activities, doing things with friends, can build friendships, and even make them easier.

"I've learned," Jimmy told me, "that sometimes it's easier to talk when you're doing something, some kind of activity, even if it's just walking along together, or even playing video games. I play a lot of video games on the Xbox, and I've gotten closer to a lot of people I wasn't that close with before because when I play with them, even though we're not physically hanging out together, we're talking together. Before Covid, I could go over to a friend's house and we'd play video games together, but now, during Covid, it's a great way to connect when you're not in person. Of course, you can connect with people on the phone, texting, or FaceTime, and it's a good way to stay in touch, but I feel like sometimes those conversations get kind of stale. But playing video games with friends, you can talk about the game, talk about what's happening, and then you can get into talking about important things more easily. Like gaming together gives you an easy way to start talking, even if it's about the game, and that can lead to more serious conversations."

IT'S IMPORTANT TO HAVE FRIENDS FROM DIFFERENT PARTS OF YOUR LIFE

If all your friends were from just one part of your life, your opportunities to broaden your experience would be very limited. Just think: If your only friends were your school friends, most of your experiences would be similar. But if you have some friends who don't go to your school, you have a wider set of experiences to bring to each other. For many kids, having school friends, neighborhood friends, camp friends, or friends from a club, recreation center, sports team, or someplace where they've lived before who don't all share the same experiences provides a much more diverse sphere of socialization and enjoyment than a single source of friends might yield.

For Grace, having an expansive network of friends had emotional benefits as well. "I think," said Grace, "that keeping all your friends in one little friend group just creates more drama than necessary. One reason is that every group of friends is bound to sometimes have their spats, and if your only friends are in that group, you don't have anyone outside of it to go to. I think that would be really isolating. So having friends from different groups, that you can go to about different things, can be really important. Having separate friends, friends who are not all in the same group—not necessarily by choice, but just because that's how it is—can be really helpful; it's like an escape, almost, from everything."

REAL FRIENDS ARE THERE WHEN YOU NEED THEM

Perhaps the greatest expectation we have of our friends is that they will be there when we need them. As with all other aspects of real friendship, that expectation should go both ways: we want our

Jimmy found that doing activities with others can help start conversations.

friends to be there for us when we need them, and we want to be there for our friends when they need us.

"One thing I've learned," said Kate, "Is that friendship is very much based not only on a common interest, but on helping each other out. You can enjoy all sorts of friends and acquaintances, but the true test of a friendship is when you need something, like emotional support, your true friends are always there. And that's how I know when someone might drop off my 'best friends' category, and I see that they're just a casual friend. The people who support me emotionally are the ones I tend to gravitate to, and stick with longer, because they not only make me happy when we're having fun, but they lift me up when I'm not feeling as good. And I want to be able to do that for them as well."

8

HOW A PANDEMIC
AFFECTED FRIENDSHIPS

The devastating, worldwide impact of the Covid-19 pandemic has been felt in every area of life. Fears about the virus, job losses, school closures, economic suffering, and political and social strife have affected everyone, of any age, from every walk of life, and from everywhere across the globe. Not least among the difficult issues we have all faced because of the pandemic is the resulting loneliness, isolation, and distortion of our daily routines, which has shaken the very foundations of who we are, how we relate to each other, and how we think about the future.

For teens, whose lives were no less disrupted than those of adults, one of the greatest challenges has been the almost complete shutdown of socialization, of the ability to make friends, see friends, enjoy activities with friends, and "stretch their wings" as they navigate the transition between childhood and adulthood. Adolescence and young adulthood are fraught with hormonal changes that affect emotions, body image, relationships, and thinking; the multitude of fears about the virus, the requisite social distancing, and the tumultuous changes in daily life that the pandemic imposed were especially hard on young people poised on the verge of adulthood.

So how did young people cope? How did they manage to make new friends, keep old friends, and deal with the changes in their lives that the pandemic entailed? What, if anything, changed about the way they think about friendship, and how did they keep their social engagement alive?

SMALL, SOCIALLY DISTANCED GET-TOGETHERS BECAME A WAY OF LIFE

For Tali, seeing her best friend in person was a tremendous relief after months of isolation. "It was huge for me to finally see my best friend Sofia. I finally saw her late in the summer, months after school went remote and we all had to stay home. When the weather was still good she came over to my house, and we did a socially distanced dinner, outdoors, which was really fun. She's coming over again for my birthday; the weather should be better by then, and I'm having four friends over and we're having another socially distanced dinner. I'd love to go out to a movie, but I'm not sure my parents will think that's a good idea yet."

In Jordi's words, "The best thing about friendship is the company. That wasn't such an issue when we were all in school together, but during the pandemic, when people—parents—are mostly working from home, even if we're all in the same apartment, sometimes parents can be busy and don't want to be bothered. And when I'm home now, if I'm not going to school and I'm doing school remote, sometimes I finish my work early, and it can get a little bit lonely, like if my parents have meetings and are busy with their stuff. So I would really love a friend to talk to, hang out with in person. But if I can't have that, at least I can see my friends on FaceTime or Zoom. And I can't wait till things open up more and we can actually be together, even if we still have to take precautions. But the biggest thing I miss about all this? Having a friend to hug."

TECHNOLOGY CHANGED THE WAY TEENS INTERACT

One significant change the pandemic has surely brought is that staying connected with friends and peers became less possible to do in person but more important to do online—whether that was texting or being on FaceTime, Snapchat, Zoom, or other social media platforms. As Katherine Cusumano wrote in a recent article in the *New York Times*, "Writing letters, sending voice memos, scheduling phone or video dates—keeping in touch during the pandemic doesn't have to be impersonal, even if it's not in person."[1] How does that change the dynamics of friendship—and how does the increasing amount of "screen time" affect young people?

Even before the pandemic, researchers were looking into how social media usage affects the mental health of young people and pointed out several areas where screen time can have both positive and negative effects on teens. Some studies have shown that kids might experience more negative feelings about such things as body image or the fear of missing out, as well as developing a kind of addiction to cell phone usage. But there is also evidence that the benefits of Internet access include such things as increased media literacy, enhanced creativity, and a sense of belonging, as well as the ability to reach out to crisis lines or other sources of help.[2] For better or worse, though, the pandemic demanded that much more of life took place online—school as well as socializing. With the personal distancing that the pandemic imposed, maintaining personal connections online—whether with schoolmates or close friends— became a necessary and unavoidable element in everyone's life.

During the pandemic, young people became adept at finding ways to stay connected with their friends. Old routines were revised to enable those connections, and new routines were developed.

"I always used to love to hang out with my friends," said Jordi, "and we used to have these awesome sleepovers, when we stay up all night, eat ice cream, and laugh about everything. Okay, so that's not something we've been able to do in ages, but I did find another way we can kind of get together. There's this thing called Netflix

Teleparty, where we can watch the same movie and do text chat about it at the same time—or just put each other on mute if we don't feel like talking. It's not exactly like being in the same room, on the same couch, but it's been a great way to have fun and feel like we're together."

And, as Sylvia pointed out, "There are so many platforms that my friends and me could use, like Zoom. I guess FaceTime is like the go-to thing, the most used app. We could use phone calls, and we do sometimes actually call each other, but then you just hear each other; you don't get to see each other. So for us, it's mostly FaceTime."

For Henry, Google Hangouts helps him stay connected to his best friend Jake. "We've been able to do some sports because they are outdoors, and we're getting back to in-person school. But since we can't really hang out together otherwise, Google Hangouts works."

Staying in touch by phone is still a much-used option. As Judith said, "Some of my friends never check their email, but they do answer their phones. And sometimes that's just the best way to stay in touch."

Sylvia finds that she stays in touch with friends on other electronic platforms. "My friends and I talk on Discord, this online chatting thing, a lot. I've actually made a new friend on Discord, because we were both on a server with people who shared our interests. I've never met her in person, because she lives in Texas and I'm in the East, but we've talked on the phone and text a lot. We also use FaceTime, of course. And before Halloween a bunch of my friends were able to come over to our backyard, where we set up chairs so we were all far apart, and we watched *Corpse Bride*. We also Rickrolled the neighbors and played "Never Gonna Give You Up" by Rick Astley about thirty times in a row. It was crazy, but the neighbors were pretty good about it and thought it was funny. I think they were cutting us a little slack because it was Halloween, and the pandemic."

For Kate, "Because we obviously can't be in the same place, my friends and I use a website called Scener, where we can watch the same thing at the same time. The best part is that only one person has to have Scener; they can start it, pick something to watch, and send out an invite to friends to watch at the same time. There's a chat feature, so you can literally just be on a call and watch the show. It's not as great as being together but it's better than being alone."

COVID CHANGED THE WAY TEENS THOUGHT ABOUT FRIENDSHIP

In his *New York Times* article "Do We Even Need Friends after the Pandemic?,"[3] author Alex Williams looks at how the dislocation of our social lives caused by the pandemic affects the way we think about friendship. He considers whether the narrower social circles the pandemic restrictions forced on us are on an inherently more human scale than the dozens and dozens of social media "friendships" so many people have grown used to. And he found that some people are reconsidering their circles of friendship and finding themselves winnowing out less valuable friendships as they retain and strengthen more enduring ones. The teens I spoke to echoed some of his findings.

As Grace recounted, "The pandemic was definitely hard on friendships. It has definitely shown me who I was closest with. Who I kept in touch with was actually very surprising to me; there were some people who I thought I would stay in good touch with, but we just didn't. And I realized that Covid definitely made me put more effort into my friendships, which I think has made me a better friend in general. Everyone went through their weird times, and it was like some friends just disappeared and maybe then reappeared. But I think staying on FaceTime or Zoom was very helpful for everybody."

Kate explained how Covid affected her friendships. "Covid made me realize what true friends are. Especially last year, when we didn't have that easy access to friends that being in school gives you, I found that your true friends were the first ones to reach out to you. It was the kids who worked to keep a relationship, a conversation, going who would reach out to you, or respond positively if you reached out to them. I think that people who want to be around you will make an effort to be around you. And if you demonstrate that you want to be around them, it cements the relationship. With this Covid thing, it's made a difference in my friend group, because we've been trying to find creative ways to have fun and still be safe and see each other. I FaceTime at least one person every night, to stay socially active I'd guess you'd say. And as hard as it can be at times, we always find a real way to make friendship work."

KATE'S STORY

For me, what came to light is that it's not going to stay this way forever; eventually, we'll move past the way things are now. I remember the early days of the pandemic, when I was really freaked out; school was hard, and weird, and it seemed like the first focus had to be getting school back on track. I still talked with my friends, but not as much as I could have, and I felt that's okay, you don't have to talk to people 24/7 to stay close. Then after a while, when things started to settle down, I started to realize who my real friends are, the ones I really wanted to see; they were the ones I knew that it didn't matter how long I didn't see them, they were still a big part of my life. We were finally able to get together during the summer. My best friends came over to my house, and we sat outside on my driveway, far apart, and we talked a bit, and just hung out together; it was all that our parents allowed. We stayed outside as long as we could; it just felt so good to be together. Seeing each other in person you can really connect with people more; facial expressions, body language, or—and this is what we couldn't do during Covid—hugging, or play fighting, horsing around, that kind of thing. It's just that we're happier together; we're friends.

* * *

The pandemic was a tough time for Kate, especially when it came to staying in contact with her friends. However, it helped her learn who her real friends are.

For Tali, going to camp during the pandemic posed both challenges and pleasures. "The summer was strange, because I went to camp during Covid, and in a lot of ways it was really hard because it was so different from other summers at camp. Everything was socially distant, and a lot of the things we would normally have done we couldn't do. Still, it's kind of nice now to be able to go back to that place in my mind, and think about when I was at camp, and we didn't have to wear masks around our friends. It's been harder to maintain a friendship with my school friends during the year, because all the time we were doing remote school, I wasn't really having the chance to talk with them every day like I would have during in-person school. And with some of my friends, whose parents are strict about their phone use, I haven't been able to talk with them on the phone as much as I'd like to. So actually being able to be together with my friends at camp, even if it was during the pandemic, was really great."

AND YOUNG PEOPLE ARE LOOKING FORWARD TO RESUMING OLD PLEASURES

"Sleepovers!" That was Cipi's quick answer when I asked what she looked forward to most after restrictions are lifted. "We used to have these huge sleepovers, and watch TV all night!" For many kids with whom I spoke, sleepovers were one of the biggest things they missed. The freedom to stay up all night together, laugh, eat junk food, and watch videos together for hours was something they said they missed time and time again. And the benefits of sleepovers are not to be understated; as writer Lydia Denworth wrote in a recent piece in the *New York Times*, "The good old-fashioned sleeping-bags-on-the-couch, talking-into-the-wee-hours sleepover is one of the last chunks of unscheduled, unstructured time in the lives of many of today's modern kids."[4] Even if Netflix Teleparties and similar platforms allow group movie watching even when kids are not together, there is nothing like a real sleepover to bond friendships.

TIPS ON MAKING AND KEEPING GOOD FRIENDS

Hopefully, this book has given you some insight into what makes friendship such a special relationship, as well as how to approach friendship, recognize good friendships, and make friendships stronger and more long lasting. The young people with whom I spoke had some very thoughtful insights and suggestions for how to make—and keep—good friends, which they wanted to share.

SOMETIMES ALL IT TAKES TO MAKE A FRIEND IS TALKING TO SOMEONE

In Jordi's experience, to make a friend, sometimes all you have to do is just talk to someone. As she recounts, "I went to tryouts for the volleyball team in the first week of school. We had to line up by twos, and go and hit the ball, and I was teamed up with this other girl, so I started talking with her. And then we stuck together throughout the tryouts, and when we came out of the gym where the tryouts were, we saw her mom and my mom talking together, which we thought was kind of funny. And our friendship took off from there, and she became one of my best friends."

TIPS FOR MAKING FRIENDS

SAY "Hi"

STAY IN TOUCH

JOIN A TEAM OR CLUB

USE CONVERSATION STARTERS

BE FRIENDLY TO SOMEONE SHY

LISTEN

And Judith pointed out, "This may sound overly confident, but if you think you want to meet someone who might turn out to be a friend, just go up and say hi. It's hard to do, but just do it—you'll be happy you did."

Judith had some other thoughts about opening up a conversation with a potential friend. "Always be nice to the other person you'd like to be friends with, but don't expect that they're going to like you just because you have things in common. Always listen to the other person, and see if you can learn more about them."

And Ben pointed out how kindness and humor can help ease the awkwardness of talking to someone new. "I always think that if you're trying to start up a conversation with someone new, one good way to do it is to offer them a compliment, say something nice about something they are wearing, or something they did. And joke with them! Get the friendly banter going; use a little humor; try to be funny without pushing it too hard."

As Kate acknowledged, "Sometimes making friends can be really hard at first. I know that in my age group, conversation can be hard, especially keeping conversation flowing. We're all teenagers, and we all feel awkward—at least a lot of the time. My best advice to people who do feel awkward about starting a conversation is— hard as it seems at times—just talk to someone new like you'd talk to someone you already know; that's worked for me. Another thing I'd suggest, and it may sound weird, is to have some conversation starters ready, things you can say to open a conversation. Like asking someone if they listen to a band you like, or like a show you like, or if they're taking a certain class or like the teacher. If you get used to starting that way, you actually get better, less awkward, at doing it. It's like having tools in your toolkit. And then when they answer, you actually get a conversation going, and it becomes less awkward when you find you have things to talk about."

Max described how getting into casual conversation over a common interest can lead to friendship. "One time, when I was on the bus to school, I was reading a book, and this person sits next to me and was looking over my shoulder to see what I was reading. And after I while, when I could tell he was reading over my shoulder, I asked him if he wanted to read the book at the same time. And that's how we became friends. We ended up reading together on the bus every Wednesday and Friday on the way to school. He was new that year, and I saw he was interested in what I was reading. Some kids might have been shy about asking a new kid to read with them. And I think to become a friend, you have to learn what other people like and see if you can relate to that."

RECOGNIZING AND ACKNOWLEDGING YOUR SHYNESS OR SOCIAL DISCOMFORT

For some—if not most—teens, feeling socially awkward is routine. The idea of just going up to someone and introducing yourself can be terrifying to some kids; fears of rejection, of being teased, or just ignored, make taking action to make a friend almost impossible. But recognizing your social discomfort, and thinking about your feelings about it, can sometimes open up possibilities. Sylvia described her mixed feelings about dealing with her social discomfort.

"I am not the best person at making friends," said Sylvia. "Whenever I'm at a party or in some group like that, I'm the person in the room who's sitting awkwardly alone in the corner. If I do happen to have a friend there, and they don't know anyone either, then we sometimes both end up sitting awkwardly in the corner. Even if there is someone I know there, and they have other friends at the party they could introduce me to, I'm still probably going to be sitting in the corner, because I just don't feel ready to go up to them and get into a conversation. But I know that if I'm in a situation where I'm kind of forced to interact socially, I can do it, and they probably won't know how socially inept I feel. Especially if someone else is crazy extroverted, and they go out of their way to engage with me, then it actually makes me feel kind of happy, unless they're really acting strange and drawing attention to us. But usually it will make me happy, because they draw me in, and I don't have to go up to some stranger and awkwardly say hi. It really depends on the situation, and if it pushes me totally beyond my comfort."

But, as Grace pointed out, "You're never as awkward as you think you are. People are always scared about going up to people, because 'Oh, they'll think I'm weird, or they'll think I'm awkward and shy,' but in all honesty, shyness is not a bad thing; people just want to make friends, the same as you do; we're all in the same boat. Everyone feels a little bit awkward, everyone's worried about how people see them, but in the end, everyone just has the same common goal: to meet people who will understand you, people that you'll like."

Another suggestion from Jordi was, "If you're shy, don't be afraid to let your shyness show, because the person you're talking to could be just as shy. Don't be afraid to show your true qualities, even if that's being shy. If you're someone who doesn't think they have the ability to talk to someone, maybe just try to say hi, how's your day going, or something like that—and keep it going, don't let the conversation just drop and disappear. It can be a little hard sometimes to keep it in the air, but keep it going, so you have a chance to get to know each other a little."

JORDI'S STORY

Sometimes all it takes to find a friend is to start up a conversation. I met one of my good friends at a swimming pool, first day of swim team. We were both there just waiting for the coach to let us into the pool, and she happened to be sitting next to me. I was feeling self-conscious and lonely, because it was my first day there, and I was so scared, because everyone was older than me, and I was sure I wouldn't fit in. I hadn't really gone swimming much—well, I'd been swimming for years, but I wasn't really the best, I just swam in a tiny pool not meant for competitive swimmers, and I was new to this whole thing, and it was so scary. So I was feeling overwhelmed, but I said hi to her and "What's your name?," that kind of thing, and then I just confessed, "It's my first day. I'm new to this kind of

After noticing the boy next to him reading over his shoulder, Max offered to share his book. They discovered they were interested in the same books and ended up reading together on the bus.

stuff." And she told me a little about how things worked, then we walked to the pool together, and we started screaming when we jumped in because the water was freezing. And then we just kept swimming, and we couldn't talk because you can't talk when you swim. But every time we finished our laps, we would talk to each other about how we're so tired, things like that, things that we could both relate to. And then we kept seeing each other at swim team, and we always had something to talk about, and we turned out to be great friends. And I wouldn't probably have gotten to know her if I didn't break the ice by saying hi."

* * *

Judith echoed Jordi's advice: "Try not to be nervous when you are meeting someone new. Because if there's someone you want to be friends with, and they're standing alone, chances are they probably also want a friend, and they may be nervous about it, too." And Judith had some creative advice for those who might find it hard to talk to someone new. "One way not to be scared about talking to someone new is to pretend that you're talking into a mirror, not to them; you'll actually be talking to a real person, but in your head you can kind of make them disappear, but still be pretending to have a conversation with them as though you're having one in a mirror. If you can tell yourself, 'They're not here, I'm just having a conversation with myself,' you can talk and be less shy. Otherwise, use the very old trick of imagining them in their underwear—it will make them seem less intimidating."

And Max put it more simply: "If you're afraid of making friends, then just try to face that fear. And once you face that fear, then the fears go away, and you can make friends easily."

TRY TO MAKE AS MANY FRIENDS AS POSSIBLE

Not long ago, while studying primate behavior, anthropologist and psychologist Robin Dunbar came up with a theory about the number of people an average person could have in their social group before it became too unwieldy. That number was approximately 150—now known as "Dunbar's number." In his work, while that number relates to casual acquaintances, he went on to study different levels of friendships, such as close friends, or friends you would turn to when you need sympathy, or your most intimate friends, and found a numeric pattern to each of these levels of friendship—in other words, how many friends of each level a person could handle. [1]

Whether or not there is an ideal number of friends, most of the kids I spoke with felt that having multiple friends was a good thing and had some thoughts about how best to do that. Cipi, for example, gave some suggestions about making multiple friends. "Try and make as many friendships as possible. I know some people feel intimidated at the idea of making friends, and they don't do anything about it, basically sitting alone and freezing. But you have to try to start friendships, and you have to branch out, and don't be afraid to make as many friendships as possible with people. One way to do that is to go out for as many clubs as possible, like after-school clubs. I'm in a lot of clubs, and that's where you form a lot of bonds. The same thing with teams; I'm on the travelling debate team, and we go to tournaments and competitions, and I have some friends on the team, because on the debate team we have to rely on each other, so that friendship is born."

IF YOU DON'T BECOME FRIENDS WITH SOMEONE, DON'T TAKE IT PERSONALLY

Trying to make friends doesn't always work out the way we hope it will. And when that happens, Kate pointed out, don't take it personally.

"You never know how things will turn out," said Kate, "When you're trying to make a new friend. Some kids are so afraid of being rejected that they won't even try to make friends with someone. I would say, in the nicest way possible, just take action and do what you want to do. Nobody reasonable would get mad at you for just trying to make friends. So if you ask them to hang out, they're

Making friends in the pool.

probably going to say yes—so my best advice would be to just ask them. But don't take it personally if they say no. It probably means that they're just not the right person for you—or they're just busy. So maybe ask another time, or try another approach, and see how it goes. Don't be afraid to ask people to do 'friend' things with you; most people would be pleased to be asked. And finally, I would say there's one thing that really helps me when I'm bothered by some interaction with someone: I just remind myself that it's not going to matter in a few years. Why stress over something if it's not going to matter in a few years—or even in a few weeks. If the issue doesn't disappear, well, it's still not going to scar you for life."

TRUST IS AN IMPORTANT PART OF FRIENDSHIP

Time and again, the teens I spoke with highlighted the importance of trust as a part of friendship. In Grace's words, "Make sure that you are there for your friends as much as they are there for you, and always be reliable. Knowing that your friend trusts you is a big deal, and you have to be careful not to betray that trust. With some people, trust is earned, and I think that especially with people like that, knowing that they can trust you is very important. Make sure that you keep that trust."

DON'T GET INVOLVED WITH THE MEAN KIDS

It's sometimes easy to find yourself in a group that turns out to be mean, Cipi points out, but, she says, "You don't want to get involved with mean girls. There's often something like a mean girl trio, or a clique of three or four people, and they try to be bossy, sassy, and cooler than cool, and I say, stay away from them. They might think that you have the potential to be one of them, and they'll try to get you to join their group, but you want to stay away from that. Sometimes they're just looking to make trouble, and you don't need it. If you're the new kid in school who doesn't yet have friends, they might see you sitting alone at a lunch table—lunch seems to be always the classic place, that cafeteria thing. And those mean girls might pretend to be your friends, cause they know you're desperate to make friends, and they'll try to sweet talk you to join them. But it's like the movie *Mean Girls*, kind of like that. Those mean girls will try to get you to join their group, but stay away from that. That never turns out good. They can end up teasing, mocking, even bullying you, because you thought they were your friends."

BE GENUINE

The importance of being yourself, not hiding behind a façade, and being genuine were sentiments I heard echoed by many of the teenagers with whom I spoke.

"Be who you are," Henry offered, "because that is who you are, not who other people want you to be."

Hattie agreed: "I think it's very important to be yourself, especially when you're meeting new people. People are more likely to be attracted to the real you: they don't want a façade, a persona that you're trying to put on."

"Just be yourself," Sara echoed. "If you're putting on a false front, you might end up becoming friends with someone who doesn't really know who you are. And then the friendship will fail, and you'll have to start all over again. I think it's really important to just be yourself."

And Ben put it simply: "Be yourself. No one wants a pretender. Don't use an alter ego. People want real people, so be yourself. That true self is *your* self."

REMEMBER THAT SOMETIMES IT PAYS TO "GO ALONG TO GET ALONG"

Although being honest and genuine was high on the list of desirable traits of everyone I spoke with, sometimes finding a way to fit in means making slight adjustments to your own true self. Cipi described a moment where she found it worthwhile to pretend an interest in something she cared little about: "Before Covid, when I started a new school, I felt like I was pretty good at making friends. I like clubs and other activities, and so that made it easy to make friends. But now, when we are doing school remote, on screens, there's no time like lunch, or recess, or after-school teams and clubs, where you can actually communicate with kids easily and get to make friends. So when a couple of the girls started chatting about how they like this very popular Korean pop band called BTS, even though I'm not really that into BTS—they're okay, but I'm not so crazy about them as these girls are—I kind of went along, and oohed and aahed over them, like, 'Oh yeah, they're totally amazing,' to kind of fit in. So I think sometimes you kind of need to maybe exaggerate something a little—it's not lying, it's just sort of identifying with them a little, to get them to accept you. And it worked out, and I really like those girls, and we're pretty friendly now."

GIVE PEOPLE A CHANCE TO REDEEM THEMSELVES

Henry had some good advice for situations where you may have felt wronged or hurt by a friend. "If you really want to be a good friend to other people, you should always give them a chance to redeem themselves. Even if they've done something that you didn't like, give them a chance to apologize and try to make it up to you."

AND RECOGNIZE YOU MIGHT BE PART OF THE PROBLEM

Sylvia pointed out that it's important to recognize when you might be the one who's causing issues in a friendship. "One of the most important things is just to be nice to your friends, and make sure that if you're joking around, you make sure that it doesn't turn into insulting someone. And don't say things that will drive other people crazy, especially not over and over again. I was doing that, and my friends really came down hard on me about it—I thought I was being funny, but they just thought I was being incredibly annoying, and they really blasted me for it. I won't do that again.

REMEMBER THAT FRIENDSHIP DOESN'T HAPPEN INSTANTLY

Sometimes we are so anxious to cultivate friends that we expect friendship to happen instantly. Sometimes it does—but most often, it takes time to really get to know someone and develop that special feeling that is friendship. A professor at the University of Kansas studied just how long it takes to develop a friendship and found that it takes about fifty hours to move from being an acquaintance to being a casual friend, about ninety hours to go from being a casual friend to being considered a friend, and another two hundred hours until you consider someone a close friend.[2]

As Judith says, "If you don't make friends with someone right away, don't be surprised, because it takes a while to actually build up friendships with people. Sometimes I've made friends in two minutes, because sometimes you 'get' somebody right away, and you click. But sometimes it takes a while to get to know someone well enough to realize, 'Well, you're really like me!' And then it is kind of like climbing up a ladder, where at first it's like you're on the bottom, not really knowing the person, then you're halfway up, where you're saying hi when you see them occasionally, maybe play handball with them sometimes, and then you reach the top of the ladder where you're best friends."

Over the years, Grace found herself starting at several different schools. "Something I've learned, especially from moving around schools, is that sometimes the first friends you make aren't going to stick with you, for whatever reason. And it can take a little bit of time to find people you really connect with, people you really like. Usually the first people I meet are great 'starting friends,' but as you get to know other people you'll find people you'll have so much more in common with, who will understand you better. So if you don't make friends at first, that just might mean you haven't found the right people yet."

When Kate had to move far away from her first home, she found that making new friends wasn't as easy as she'd hoped. "Where I moved to turned out to be a very different environment than I was used to. At first it was really hard, and kind of rocky. I'd meet someone and think we could become friends, and then we didn't. Or I thought I was friends with someone, and then I wasn't. Because it was kind of hard to find where I fit in. But eventually I did find people. So what I would suggest to kids who are going someplace new, whether it's a neighborhood or school, is—as corny as it sounds—join clubs, join sports. That's what I did, and that's how I met my best friend. I met her through lacrosse. I don't play anymore, but that's how I met her, and we became close friends very quickly, because I'd see her in school and then in sports, so it worked pretty well. We found that we immediately had an interest in common."

"What I would say to kids who are trying to find friends," Jimmy suggested, "is not to be discouraged if you're not included in a friend group you want to join, or make friends immediately with someone. It may just mean that they're not the right ones for you. It's important to find friends even if they're not the ones you expected to find, and it's important to keep trying throughout your whole life."

DEMONSTRATE FRIENDSHIP

"I'm sometimes shy," said Morgan, "so I understand why some kids are too shy to make friends. But I figure if they got used to having a friend, they would know what it's like and be able to make some more. And if they don't have siblings, they might not be used to the kind of casual give and take kids can have. So when I see someone who seems to be in that situation, I've gone up to them and tried to open a conversation, just said hi, and tried to include them with my friends, so they could get the feeling of joyfulness of having a friend and being close to them, and then maybe they would not be so shy."

Emily put it slightly differently. "There are some kids who try too hard to make friends, and I think that it sometimes backfires. I think the best way to make friends is to just be nice; don't focus on trying to be friends with one specific person, but overall, just be nice to everyone. Then people will think, 'Oh, she's so nice! I'd like to be friends with her!'"

As Kate suggested, sometimes just greeting people in a friendly way can be a step toward making a friend. "Having moved to a new school in a whole new neighborhood, I didn't know anybody," Kate reflected. "But when I started recognizing kids who were in my class, I started to say hi to them when I passed them in the hall or the neighborhood, and I always got a hi back. I know that when people said hello to me, it made me happy. I don't really know why. It was just the recognition; it felt like they were acknowledging, 'I value you enough to say hello to you,' and that meant a lot, especially when I didn't know many people. So I think it's something you should always do, just say hi to people you know. It can open a path to friendship."

FIND PEOPLE WHO SHARE YOUR INTERESTS

Jimmy explained: "I would say to kids who would like to find friends, to look around and see who are the people with whom you have a lot of similarities, because those are the people you'll have a lot to talk about with. For instance, I love sports, so the people who I have a lot to talk about with are people who love sports. I think that, in my case, all my friends are similar to me in that they all like sports, and we always have things to talk about. We're also similar in other ways: like our parents all have similar values, we're all smart, we're all in honors math, and stuff like that. And I think that the similarities are what bring us together, so we hang out a lot together, and being together so much makes us even closer."

Jimmy continued, "Sometimes you have to go out of your way to try and make friends. Like if you go to a new school, most kids who are already at that school for a while probably have their own group of friends, and, if you're new, you have to look for a group to join. I think extracurricular activities, like sports, are a really good way to meet people, because you'll all have something in common. And even though I personally don't do theater, I know a lot of the theater kids end up being tight friends, like kids who go to math camps and study math all the time become good friends. I think a lot of friendship is about having common interests, so if you find a group that shares your interest, you can make friends in that group."

Tali pointed out that it can be easy to find interests in common if you talk about favorite TV shows. "If you're trying to make friends, sometimes all it takes is finding a TV show you both love. When I first met Katy, it turned out that there's a TV show we both watch all the time. We were able to talk a lot about that—and that's a good way to make a friendship stronger, because you can reach out to that person more, talk to them more."

SHOW SUPPORT FOR YOUR FRIENDS

"You should definitely have your friend's back," said Sara. "There's a lot of rivalry in school, especially when you're in class, and I think it's really important to support your friend. Be on their side. But if they do or say something you disagree with, be honest with them, but do it in a nice way. And be careful about disagreeing with them in front of other kids; maybe just talk with them privately if you don't agree with them."

WORK HARD TO KEEP GOOD FRIENDS

For Morgan, the song "Make New Friends, but Keep the Old" resonates. "Even if you move away, or your friends switch to another school, don't forget the friends who were really nice to you, and try to forget the people who haven't been so nice to you. It can be hard to hold on to your friends sometimes, especially if they move away, or they go to a different school and you don't get to see them that often. But if you let them go, it can make you sad, and you'll regret that you didn't work harder to keep up the friendship. So call, write, text, whatever it takes, so that even while you might have new friends, you still keep the old friendships going."

Henry also reflected on how to maintain friendships. "I think that if you want to be a better friend, just generally be kind to people. And also, if you really want to become a better friend, try to be more interactive, try to be helpful, try to listen. It's really not that complicated."

One valuable thing that Sara pointed out is how important it is to maintain contact with your friends. "Especially during Covid, when you can't see your friends in person," Sara said, "I think you need to make sure you stay in touch with them, even if you have to work at it. For instance, if your friend leaves you a message to call, you can't just say, 'Oh, I don't really feel like talking to Andrea tonight,' because then you're not being there for a friend."

Kate moved across the state a few years ago and described her experience trying to keep up with old friends. "When we moved from Long Island to Buffalo, I didn't know anyone in Buffalo, but I had lots of friends on Long Island. And one thing I've noticed about friendship, especially if you've moved away, is not to be afraid to just reach out to people; in all honesty, they're not going to get mad if you just reach out with a 'Hey, how's it going?' once in a while. I know that when my old friends text me, my response is, "OMG, you texted me!' and it makes me feel so great that they haven't forgotten me. And it goes both ways; I feel, 'Hey, I used to talk to you all the time, so reach out to me,' even if it's Happy Birthday or something. And it's like, 'OMG, I remember them!' and 'OMG, they remember me too!' And my best friend from Long Island is still my best friend to this day. We don't talk as much as we used to, because, obviously, I'm not there, but we still talk, quite a bit, and that's because both of us have made a big effort to keep up with each other. Because friendship is a very two-sided thing. You can't have one person trying to make it a thing and then one person not. And if it comes to that, if they just don't want to work to keep a friendship, you're better off with better friends—because there *are* better friends out there. That's also something that's hard to remember, but there's somebody out there who likes you, and there'll be someone out there who doesn't like you—and that's okay. Not everybody has to like you; not everybody has to be your friend. But you *will* find good friends, and, if you work at it, you will keep them."

As Tali pointed out, it's important to be thoughtful and flexible with your friends. As she commented perceptively, "Think about what your friend wants, instead of just what you might want. Sometimes it's important to either go along with what they want or find a way to compromise. A friendship has to be balanced, so it's not always one-sided."

DON'T JUDGE OTHERS BY FIRST IMPRESSIONS OR OUTWARD APPEARANCE

Henry made a very good point: "One thing I've learned is, don't judge people by their outsides but by their insides. You may think someone is weird because of the way they dress, or their gender, or their social status. And I've found that you can't judge someone by the way they look; you need to get to know who they are, and what their real self is like. That's what matters."

And, in Grace's experience, "Someone who you might not have been close friends with at first could turn out to be the best person you'll ever meet."

PUT YOURSELF OUT THERE AND BE OPEN TO FRIENDSHIP

"Just make friends with people whom you don't know," said Kate simply. "Put yourself out there and be open to friendship. I found that people who are happy, who enjoy the people they are around, become even more attractive to other people. When someone sees that you're enjoying yourself and having fun with friends, they figure that you must be a nice person, someone people want to be friends with. I always think that if you put out a positive attitude, people will gravitate to you, and you'll have an easy time making friends."

FINALLY, LISTEN TO YOUR FRIENDS

How can you make a good friendship better? "Make sure you're listening," Grace said. "Listen to what your friend is saying. Don't just try to tell your friend what *you* want to say. Trying to talk over someone, or tell them what you think instead of listening to what they are saying, isn't just rude. It shows that you don't care enough to hear them out."

Sara voiced a similar thought about the importance of listening: "You should always be willing to listen to your friends. It's hard, sometimes, to just listen, because sometimes you just want to interject with your own thing. But before you interrupt, you should just stop, and listen, and then you can add something after they're finished. Otherwise it seems like you're not listening; you're just wanting to talk."

Emily's suggestion was even more direct: "Listen to your friends. Let them talk."

APPENDIX

Resources

As noted earlier in this book, making friends comes naturally to some people, while for others it can seem intimidating or even anxiety producing. Whether you just want to make some new friends or make more friends, or have moved somewhere new and need to start over finding friends, there are steps you can take to help smooth the process of expanding your social circle. Joining a school club, a sports team, or a national organization for teens or signing up to become a volunteer for a local or national organization can provide a ready-made circle of people about your age with similar interests to yours. The easiest place to start is through your school: check out school clubs, teams, and chapters of national organizations, and sign up to see what it's like and who you might meet. For more ideas, below is a selective list of clubs and organizations where you might find like-minded teens and—very likely—make some friends.

BOYS & GIRLS CLUBS OF AMERICA

1275 Peachtree Street NE

Atlanta, GA 30309-3506
404-487-5700
https://www.bgca.org/

Boys & Girls Clubs of America (BCGA) is a national organization of local chapters that provide voluntary after-school programs for young people with the goal of ensuring that all young people reach their full potential as productive, caring, responsible citizens.

BOY SCOUTS OF AMERICA

National Service Center
PO Box 152079
Irving, TX 75015
https://www.scouting.org/

The Boy Scouts help young people appreciate and respond to the needs of others through engagement in community service.

4-H

7100 Connecticut Avenue
Chevy Chase, MD 20815
301-961-2800
https://4-h.org/

America's largest youth development organization, 4-H provides kids with community, mentors, and learning opportunities to develop the skills they need to create positive change in their lives and communities.

FUTURE BUSINESS LEADERS OF AMERICA

312 East Walnut Street, Suite 200

Lancaster, PA 17602
800-220-2175
https://www.fbla-pbl.org/

Future Business Leaders of America (FBLA) is the high school division of the largest career student business organization in the world. FBLA inspires and prepares students to become community-minded business leaders in a global society through relevant career preparation and leadership experiences.

GIRL SCOUTS OF AMERICA

420 Fifth Avenue
New York, NY 10018
https://www.girlscouts.org/

Girl Scouts participate in community service projects both in groups and individually.

HABITAT FOR HUMANITY

285 Peachtree Center Ave NE, Suite 2700
Atlanta, GA 30303
800-422-4828
https://www.habitat.org/volunteer/near-you/youth-programs
Habit for Humanity is a nonprofit organization that helps families build and improve places to call home.

JUNIOR ACHIEVEMENT USA

One Education Way
Colorado Springs, CO 80906
719-540-8000
https://jausa.ja.org/

Junior Achievement USA is a nonprofit that inspires and prepares young people for success, with community volunteers who share their experience and serve as role models helping to positively impact young people's perceptions about the importance of education as well as critical life skills.

KEY CLUB (KIWANIS INTERNATIONAL)

3636 Woodview Trace
Indianapolis, IN 46268
https://www.keyclub.org/

High school student members of Key Club, a youth division of Kiwanis, perform acts of service in their communities. They also learn leadership skills by running meetings, planning projects, and holding elected positions at the club, district, and international levels.

LITTLE LEAGUE BASEBALL AND SOFTBALL

https://www.littleleague.org/

The first organized youth sports program in the world, today millions of young people ages four to sixteen around the world participate in Little League baseball and softball.

MODEL UN

Education Outreach Section
Department of Global Communications
United Nations Headquarters
New York, NY 10017
https://www.un.org/en/mun/

Model UN is a popular activity for those interested in learning more about how the UN operates. Hundreds of thousands of students worldwide take part every year at all educational levels. Many of today's leaders in law, government, business, and the arts—including at the UN itself—participated in Model UN as students.

NATIONAL HONOR SOCIETY

904 Association Drive
Reston, Virginia 20191-1537
703-860-0200
https://www.nhs.us/

Students in grades 10–12 who meet the requirements for membership in the National Honor Society (NHS) outlined by their school's chapter are eligible to be invited for membership. NHS elevates a school's commitment to the values of scholarship, service, leadership, and character. Chapter membership recognizes students for their accomplishments and challenges them to develop further through active involvement in school activities and community service.

NATIONAL TEEN LEADERSHIP PROGRAM

PO Box 956
Sacramento, CA 95812
800-550-1950
https://ntlp.org/

The nonprofit National Teen Leadership Program is committed to creating positive environments that empower, inspire, and educate all teens to discover and maximize their unique leadership potential and embrace the diversity and equal value of everyone.

POP WARNER LITTLE SCHOLARS

PO Box 307
Langhorne, PA 19047
215-752-2691
https://www.popwarner.com/

The oldest national youth football and cheerleading organization in the world, Pop Warner serves youth to age sixteen.

SCIENCE OLYMPIAD

2 Trans Am Plaza Drive, Suite 310
Oakbrook Terrace, IL 60181
630-792-1251
https://www.soinc.org/

In Science Olympiad competitions, teams compete in areas such as genetics, earth science, chemistry, anatomy, physics, geology, mechanical engineering, and technology, culminating in the Science Olympiad National Tournament. Emphasis is placed on active, hands-on group participation in which students, teachers, parents, principals, and business leaders bond together and work toward a shared goal.

USA HOCKEY

1775 Bob Johnson Drive
Colorado Springs, CO 80906-4090
719-576-8724
https://www.usahockey.com/

USA Hockey provides the foundation for the sport of ice hockey in America, helping young people become leaders and promoting a lifelong love of the sport, with classifications for boys, girls, and coed teams.

US YOUTH SOCCER

PO Box 1928
Frisco, TX 75034
https://www.usyouthsoccer.org/

US Youth Soccer's mission is to foster the physical, mental, and emotional growth and development of America's youth through the sport of soccer.

NOTES

1. WHAT IS FRIENDSHIP, AND WHY IS IT IMPORTANT?

1. *Merriam-Webster Dictionary*, s.v. "friend," https://www.merriam-webster.com/dictionary/friend; s.v. "friendship," https://www.merriam-webster.com/dictionary/friendship.

2. *The Epic of Gilgamesh*, trans. Maureen Gallery Kovacs, http://www.ancienttexts.org/library/mesopotamian/gilgamesh/.

3. "King David," Jewish Virtual Library, https://www.jewishvirtuallibrary.org/king-david.

4. Ruth 1:16–17, Jewish Virtual Library, https://www.jewishvirtuallibrary.org/ruth-full-text.

5. Job 2:11, Jewish Virtual Library, https://www.jewishvirtuallibrary.org/iyov-job-full-text.

6. Marcus Tullius Cicero, *How to Be a Friend*, trans. and intro. Philip Freeman (Princeton, NJ: Princeton University Press, 2018), 43.

7. Deborah Sweeney, "Friendship and Frustration: A Study in Papyri Deir El-Medina IV-VI." *Journal of Egyptian Archaeology* 84 (1998): 101–22.

8. Will Tosh, "Shakespeare and Friendship," British Library, March 15, 2016, https://www.bl.uk/shakespeare/articles/shakespeare-and-friendship.

9. Mavis Bliss, "Aristotle on Friendship and Self-Knowledge: The Friend Beyond the Mirror," *Society for Ancient Greek Philosophy Newsletter*, January 20, 2009, https://orb.binghamton.edu/sagp/344/.

10. Lydia Denworth, "How Monkeys Taught Me to Appreciate Teen Sleepovers," *New York Times*, February 4, 2020.

11. Ana Sandoiu, "Strong Friendship in Adolescence May Benefit Mental Health in the Long Run," *Medical News Today*, August 26, 2017, https://www.medicalnewstoday.com/articles/319119,

12. "Childhood Friendships May Have Some Health Benefits in Adulthood," *Psychological Science*, March 27, 2018, https://www.psychologicalscience.org/news/releases/childhood-friendships-may-have-some-health-benefits-in-adulthood.html.

13. Yang Claire Yang, Courtney Boen, Karen Gerken, Ting Li, Kristen Schorpp, and Kathleen Mullan Harris, "Social Relationships and Physiological Determinants of Longevity Across the Human Lifespan," *Proceedings of the National Academy of Sciences* 113, no. 3 (2016): 578–83, https://www.pnas.org/content/113/3/578.

2. THE DIFFERENCE BETWEEN FRIENDSHIP AND OTHER RELATIONSHIPS

1. Alex Williams, "Do We Even Need Friends after the Pandemic?," *New York Times*, March 27, 2021.

2. *Funk & Wagnalls Standard Dictionary*, s.v. "mentor" (New York: New American Library, 1980).

3. TYPES OF FRIENDSHIPS

1. Eileen Kennedy-Moore, "Imaginary Friends," *Psychology Today*, January 31, 2013, https://www.psychologytoday.com/intl/blog/growing-friendships/201301/imaginary-friends.

2. I. Seiffge-Krenke, "Imaginary Companions in Adolescence: Sign of a Deficient or Positive Development," *Journal of Adolescence* 20, no. 2 (1997): 137–54, https://pubmed.ncbi.nlm.nih.gov/9104650/.

3. "Two-Thirds of Americans Have Multigenerational Friendships," Barna, March 12, 2019, https://www.barna.com/research/multigenerational-friendships/,

4. Maria Konnikova, "The Limits of Friendship," *New Yorker*, October 7, 2014, https://www.newyorker.com/science/maria-konnikova/social-media-affect-math-dunbar-number-friendships.

5. Jeff Brown, *Flat Stanley: His Original Adventure!*, 50th anniversary ed. (New York: HarperCollins, 2013).

4. HOW DO FRIENDSHIPS HAPPEN?

1. Emma Pattee, "How to Have Closer Friendships (and Why You Need Them)," *New York Times*, November 20, 2019, https://www.nytimes.com/2019/11/20/smarter-living/how-to-have-closer-friendships.html.

2. Lydia Denworth, *Friendship: The Evolution, Biology, and Extraordinary Power of Life's Fundamental Bond* (New York: W. W. Norton, 2020), 99.

3. Karen Karbo, "Friendship: The Laws of Attraction," *Psychology Today*, November 1, 2006, https://www.psychologytoday.com/us/articles/200611/friendship-the-laws-attraction.

5. HOW DO YOU RECOGNIZE A TRUE FRIEND?

1. Kristin Hannah, *The Great Alone* (New York: St. Martin's Press, 2018), 84.

2. Hannah, *Great Alone*, 90.

6. WHEN FRIENDSHIP FAILS

1. Denworth, *Friendship*, 111.

2. Denworth, *Friendship*, 103.

8. HOW A PANDEMIC
AFFECTED FRIENDSHIPS

1. Katherine Cusumano, "Find and Keep New Friends," *New York Times*, January 23, 2021.

2. Elia Abi-Jaoude, Karline Treurnicht Naylor, and Antionio Pignatiel, "Smartphones, Social Media Use and Youth Mental Health," *Canadian Medical Association Journal* 192, no. 6 (2020): E136–E141, https://www.cmaj.ca/content/192/6/E136.

3. Williams, "Do We Even Need Friends?"

4. Denworth, "How Monkeys Taught Me."

9. TIPS ON MAKING AND
KEEPING GOOD FRIENDS

1. Konnikova, "Limits of Friendship."

2. Jeffrey A. Hall, "How Many Hours Does It Take to Make a Friend?," *Journal of Social and Personal Relationships* 36, no. 4 (2019): 1278–96, https://journals.sagepub.com/doi/full/10.1177/0265407518761225.

BIBLIOGRAPHY

Alcott, Louisa May. *Little Women.* New York: Penguin Classics, 1956.

Austen, Jane. *Pride and Prejudice.* New York: Penguin Books, 2002.

Cicero, Marcus Tullius. *How to Be a Friend.* Translated and with an introduction by Philip Freeman. Princeton, NJ: Princeton University Press, 2018.

Criswell, Patti Kelley, illustrated by Angela Martini. *Smart Girl's Guide to Friendship Troubles.* Middleton, WI: American Girl Publishing, 2003.

de Cervantes, Miguel. *Don Quixote.* Ware, UK: Wordsworth Editions, 1997.

Denworth, Lydia. *Friendship: The Evolution, Biology, and Extraordinary Power of Life's Fundamental Bond.* New York: W. W. Norton, 2020.

Elman, Natalie Madorsky, and Eileen Kennedy-Moore. *The Unwritten Rules of Friendship: Simple Strategies to Help Your Child Make Friends.* Boston: Little, Brown, 2003.

Epstein, Joseph. *Friendship: An Exposé.* Boston: Houghton Mifflin, 2006.

Hannah, Kristin. *The Great Alone.* New York: St. Martin's Press, 2018.

Henke, Emma MacLaren, illustrated by Angela Martini. *Friends Till the End? A Quiz Book for A Smart Girl's Guide to Friendship Troubles.* Middleton, WI: American Girl Publishing, 2013.

Homer. *The Iliad.* New York: Penguin Classics, 1998.

Rawitt, Jean. *Volunteering: Insights and Tips for Teenagers.* Lanham, MD: Rowman & Littlefield, 2020.

Reece, Gemma, illustrated by Katy Jackson. *The Girls' Book of Friendship: How to be the Best Friend Ever.* New York: Scholastic, 2010.

Shakespeare, William. *The Complete Works of William Shakespeare.* Ware, UK: Wordsworth Editions, 1996.

Twain, Mark. *The Adventures of Tom Sawyer.* New York: Sterling, 2004.

Way, Niobe, and Jill V. Hamm, eds. *The Experience of Close Friendships in Adolescence.* San Francisco: Jossey-Bass, 2005.

White, T. H. *The Once and Future King.* New York: Ace Books, 1987.

INDEX

ABOUT THE AUTHOR

A former executive in book publishing, marketing, public relations, and fundraising, Jean Rawitt trained in geriatric education at the Hunter/Mount Sinai Geriatrics Education Center and went on to develop volunteer programs for Mount Sinai Hospital in New York City. She serves on the Board of Birch Family Services, a leading provider of early childhood and school-age education, residential, and community services for people with autism and developmental disabilities. She is also the author of *Volunteering: Insights and Tips for Teenagers* and *A Loved One with Dementia: Insights and Tips for Teenagers*, both published by Rowman & Littlefield.